TOP TALENT
PUBLISHING

Hidden Memories

*"When we have the courage to walk into our story
and own it, we get to write the ending."*

– Brené Brown

"The scars you can't see are the hardest to heal."

– Astrid Alauda

*"Love is what we are born with. Fear is what we learn.
The spiritual journey is the unlearning of fear and
the acceptance of love back into our hearts."*

– Marianne Williamson

*"We need to remember across generations that
there is as much to learn as there is to teach."*

– Gloria Steinem

"Music can change the world because it can change people."

– Bono

*"Someone I loved once gave me a box full of darkness. It
took me years to understand that this too, was a gift."*

– Mary Oliver

*"I can be changed by what happens to me.
But I refuse to be reduced by it."*

– Maya Angelou

*"In the midst of winter, I found there was,
within me, an invincible summer."*

– Albert Camus

Praise

"In this life, pain is inevitable, but suffering is optional. According to the Buddha, the difficult circumstances in our lives do not create our suffering - rather, it is how we choose to meet our challenges that determines our happiness or despair. In this brave and vulnerable book - part memoir, part psychological/spiritual search, part self awareness guidebook - Melissa Osorio meets the truth of deeply personal betrayal and trauma. And she chooses growth and redemption over paralysis and victimhood. She skillfully avoids platitudes and does not reduce complexity to the oversimplified dichotomy of "good people and bad people." Instead, she chooses forgiveness, self compassion, and personal responsibility over blame. As part of her journey, she tackles the topic of sexuality, trust, and passion from a deep emotional and spiritual perspective, illustrating how our sexual desire is a multifaceted, dynamic aspect of self. Take this book as a call to action and choose to rewrite your story from this breath onward, as Melissa does."

– Cheryl Fraser Ph.D. Psychologist, sex therapist, & Buddhist teacher. Author of *Buddha's Bedroom – The Mindful Loving Path to Sexual Passion and Lifelong Intimacy*, Host of the Sex Love & Elephants podcast, and creator of the *Become Passion* online couples' program. DrCherylFraser.com

Praise

"Few people have written about such sensitive subject matter in such a sophisticated way. Whether you've experienced extreme trauma or know of someone who has experienced extreme trauma, this book will be of help to you."

– The Los Angeles Tribune

"Melissa fearlessly shares her personal story of trauma and triumph. I was emotionally gripped by her journey, and her resilience serves as a beacon of hope for anyone who has weathered the storms of life."

– Dr. Neeta Bhushan, Host of The Brave Table, Author of 5x Award Winning Book, That Sucked Now What.

"This deep and introspective description of Melissa's journey through traumatic and unsettled developmental years of her childhood and young adulthood is a roadmap to all people, young and old, on how to use life's experiences to one's advantage. All of Melissa's breakthroughs and victories are cheered as the reader connects with every descriptive line, every subtle, yet poetic inuendo on her path to success and person enlightenment. I recommend this book exclusively to those who wish to see the strength they possess within, and often brought to light from pain, into a world of self-connection and true healing. Melissa invites the reader to never underestimate the moment they are in. To live in the exact moment of life, and choose effort and perseverance to lift up the self into a horizon of infinite possibilities."

– Jeffrey L. McNairy, Psy.D., M.P.H., Chief Medical Officer, Rythmia Life Advancement Center

Copyright

Hidden Memories:

Discover What's Blocking You from Life and Love

Library of Congress 2023919571

Paperback ISBN 978-1-959473-03-9

Hardback ISBN 978-1-959473-02-2

MELISSA_OSORIO_REMEMBERS

www.melissa-osorio.com

Published by

TOP TALENT
PUBLISHING

HIDDEN MEMORIES

DISCOVER WHAT'S BLOCKING YOU FROM LIFE AND LOVE

A TRUE STORY

MELISSA OSORIO

Table of Contents

Special Thanks

To my Mama - All that is beautiful about me, all the strength, love, and compassion, comes from you. Thank you for the countless sacrifices you have made and the endless love you have shown me. I love you.

To Karina, Evelyn, Monica, and Julio - I'm proud of you for waging your battles. As I navigate my own challenges, I am deeply grateful to have you by my side. Your unwavering support, understanding, and love have been an anchor.

To Miles - Your soul shines so brightly. Thank you for giving me a second chance. Your kindness, empathy, and wisdom make me believe in a brighter and more compassionate world. I will always be your bonus mom!

To my soul sister - You are an inspiration. Thank you for sharing your light with me and with the women of the world. Your presence in my life has been a gift beyond measure, and I treasure all the fun times we have!

To my tribe and soul family - I see you. I honor you. I love you. I cherish the moments of connection we share, the deep conversations that touch our souls, and the support we offer one another as we navigate the ups and downs of life. Your love and friendship have enriched my life in ways I could never have imagined.

Special Thanks

To Adam, Bono, The Edge, and Larry - Thank you for the incredible music you create; it has profoundly impacted my life. Being at your shows helped me feel alive before I came to life.

To Rythmia - Thank you for providing a safe space where I could explore my emotions, confront my fears, and heal the wounds that had been lingering within me.

To David - Thank you for cracking my heart open and for reminding me of who I am. Your presence in my life has nudged me to become the best I can be.

To Ximena and Santiago at Casa del Sol - Thank you for sharing your mountains, healing gifts, and medicine with the world. Thank you for being a sanctuary and embracing me during some of the darkest nights of my life.

To the guy with the good hair - Thank you for being the alarm clock that woke me up from my sleep.

Final Thanks - Above all, my gratitude now and forever is to God and to the infinite mystery that surrounds us. In moments of joy and celebration, I feel your presence in the laughter of loved ones, in the beauty of nature, and in the warmth of human connections. In moments of sorrow and hardship, I find solace in knowing that I am not alone and that there is a greater purpose and meaning to my experiences.

I dedicate this book to the little girl I once was.
May you always twirl and smile under the mandarin tree.

Introduction
What You Don't Know

"Knowledge is realizing that the street is one-way;
wisdom is looking both directions anyway."

– Unknown

For most of my life, I had barely any memories of my childhood. No good memories, no bad memories, just several little snippets of the first 16 years.

In fact, most of what I call memories were just images I had seen in family photos here and there. In one particular photo, I am six months old. My father carries me in his arms, and my siblings surround us. We are in our pool. We look happy. That became a memory.

Interestingly, the first memory I recovered when I was 36 years old was of a near-death experience at that very pool. The memory terrified me. It made me ask one of the questions we humans often ask: "Why?".

The question "why?" is often a challenging one. When seeking answers, it can lead you in circles or backward. However, in my case, "why" became a crucial question. It was the key to unraveling the mysteries that had plagued me for much of my life, as the answers I sought laid squarely in my past.

You might ask yourself if you can relate, but the simple truth is that you don't know what you don't know. Your past might be a mysterious puzzle waiting to be solved; events you don't remember might be vital to understanding the pieces that have shaped your life.

From Dark to Light

For many years, I walked through life as a blind person. But the thing is, I didn't know I was blind, and the people around me didn't know I was blind neither.

I didn't understand why I was so unhappy. I kept on throwing the darts and missing the bull's eye. I felt disconnected from everyone and myself.

I looked for external explanations. And after coming empty-handed, I blamed people. I was swallowed by self-pity and despair most of my life. Two years ago, the veil came off, and for the first time, I could see.

It was as if I had been living in a dark room, and suddenly, all the lights came on. It blinded me, left me gasping for air; it broke my soul.

It is said that the mythical phoenix builds a nest of twigs, and when it feels its impending death approaching, it sets the nest on fire. Much like that bird, I built my nest, and two years ago, I immolated myself. My worn-out body was consumed by the flames. From the ashes, a new Phoenix emerged. I let go of the old, embraced change, and underwent a profound transformation.

My quest for healing, knowledge, and understanding took me to many corners of the world. It introduced me to different healing modalities. It gifted me with a tribe of friends. In short, it completely changed the direction of my life for the better. Out of that quest, this book was born.

This book, crafted by an imperfect vessel, is a humble conduit for an important message that transcends its pages. As its writer, I am deeply honored that it has found its way into your hands.

Silent Killers

At first, I penned this book for myself, envisioning a younger version of me as the intended audience. But as I journeyed through the pages, I realized that the essence of childhood, with its myriad flavors, colors, and unexpected twists, resonates with us all. It became clear that these writings were meant for anyone and everyone who has experienced childhood.

In those formative years, your life was shaped by dynamic moments, both beautiful and traumatic, that left indelible imprints in your mind and body.

The nature of our experiences may vary, but their consequences are similar and linger. What you went through cast shadows over every facet of your existence, whether you're aware of it or not. Sometimes the effects are overt, while other times, they stealthily creep in like silent killers, catching you off guard.

Your Own Voyage

The backbone of this book is a journey through the ups and downs of my life. However, the pages are not just about me; they are about you. As you read them, you'll embark on a path of self-discovery. The book is, among other things, an alarm bell for those who need to wake up to a different and often more complex reality.

As you dive deep into this riveting tale of challenges, healing and empowerment, you'll learn how to break free from the shackles of past limitations and embrace life and love with newfound clarity and purpose.

The dramatic transformation of my life also invites you to explore the profound impact of psychedelics on trauma healing. The book will give you insights into alternative treatments you may have never considered.

It will introduce you to a world of expanded perspectives that can help you navigate the uncharted territories of your life. It will invite you to explore the darkest corners of your mind, where memories may lay dormant or hidden. And give you tips and tools so you can tap into your boundless reservoir of resilience.

May this book do more than touch your heart and inspire your soul. May it set ablaze a transformative spark within you, that ignites a blazing fire of profound healing and growth.

My Disclaimer

I am not a psychologist or psychiatrist. And by many accounts, I am not a mental health expert. This book is not intended to be used in place of medical advice from a medical or mental health provider. You are responsible for your choices. Several treatments mentioned use substances not currently legal in many countries, including the USA. The frequency of the treatments is neither common nor recommended.

PART 1
Unearthing My Past

"When the student is ready the teacher will appear. When the student is truly ready... The teacher will disappear."

– Tao Te Ching

My family's life resembled a complex puzzle, each piece carefully placed, forming a beautiful yet enigmatic picture. Secrets and hidden challenges were concealed by the intricate puzzle design. They were shrouded in a veil of illusion.

The first part of this book unravels some of the pieces of my past. I explore many of the formidable difficulties that profoundly impacted my childhood and adult life.

Along the way, you will meet individuals who ignited questions within me. Still, the answers remained elusive, leaving me mired in deep pain and confusion.

This poignant exploration invites you to delve into the depths of your past, unearth the untold stories that shape who you are, and find solace in the shared struggles that bind us all.

CHAPTER 1
All Over the News

*"Given the choice between the experience of
pain and nothing, I would choose pain."*

– William Faulkner

Every family has secrets. Some are more innocent than
others. The meaning you give them, how long they stay
hidden, and how these truths define you is what matters most.

I was 16 years old and it was the day of my high school
graduation. As I walked out of my room, my mom looked at
me and said, "I am proud of you." For as many times as I'd
dreamed about this day, it was nothing like I'd imagined.

I was exhausted after lying awake all night with my Mini
Doberman Pincher, Dana. She licked away the tears that rolled
down my face that night, and that had been rolling down my
face for months. It was a time of tears.

Mom was wearing a beautiful dress. She always looked
so put together. My two sisters were still getting ready, and I
remember thinking how different we all were.

I put on my tall white socks and black moccasins and
stood in front of the mirror. That girl looking back at me with
swollen, lifeless eyes was not me. It was not the girl I wanted
to be.

I wore a pleated black skirt that went down to my knees
because, as a religious girl, any shorter would have been a
sacrilege.

My brown uniform shirt with bumble bee sleeves made me look like a pompous cadaver, "This is a perfect outfit to be buried in," I thought.

Fake Funeral

I often imagined my fake funeral. I wondered what would happen if I faked my death and watched from a distance. Who would come to my funeral? Who loved me, if anyone?

My brother stepped up behind me and our eyes met in the mirror. "You look nice," he said. "Thank you," I replied. I didn't believe him. I didn't tell him I felt dead inside and that even my skin hurt. I just said, "I am ready," in my usual warrior-like tone.

The walk to the school took only five minutes. This school had been good to me. At least inside its walls, I felt in control. The teachers loved me. I was a bookworm yet everyone knew not to mess with me. I was taller than most boys, determined, and strong.

Nothing Matters Anymore

We entered the school through the front door. From the corner of my eye, I saw my photo hanging on the honor roll wall. It had been up there for six years. My older sister also saw it and asked, "Who is that cute girl?". I ignored the question and kept walking. I didn't care anymore; why would I? My father was gone now.

Once we were seated among the hundreds of other students and their families, it was time. Time for me, the valedictorian, to speak to all of them.

I stood in front of the microphone at the podium, wearing my father's oversized watch. My throat was choking down all the sentences my mind was working hard to formulate. My mind screamed: "GET IT TOGETHER, BE STRONG." I have told myself to be strong for as long as I can remember.

I could barely see the crowd; my eyes became a dam for a river of tears. Only a few sentences into my speech, the dam broke, and tears streamed down my face. My family looked back at me from the audience. They were all there. All but one person, the one that mattered most.

I felt embarrassed and powerless, but everyone in the crowd understood. They all knew what had happened. It was all over the news.

Delivering my speech during my high school graduation

CHAPTER 2
The Beginning of the End

"There is an appointed time for everything,
A time for every activity under the heavens:
A time for birth and a time to die."
– Ecclesiastes 3:1-2a

I was one year old when we took our last trip as a family. I was three years old when my eldest brother Robert was diagnosed with terminal cancer. I was 12 days short of my sixth birthday when he died at the age of twenty-one. I was nine years old when my dad finally divorced my mom, and we moved out of a very turbulent home. I was 16 years old when the world I knew changed. Twenty years later, at the age of 36, my world simultaneously collapsed and imploded.

Mom says that she always knew I would have a strong personality. I didn't allow her to lay on her back or left side during the last trimester of her pregnancy. I kicked relentlessly and demanded she lay on her right side. I wouldn't stop until she did. When I was hungry, I kicked and kicked and wouldn't stop until she ate.

Picture Perfect Family

I was born in the 1980's in Venezuela. My family was having a dinner party one January evening at our house. Around midnight, Mom, a veteran at giving birth, knew I was coming.

The night of my birth, my dad piled my four siblings and my very pregnant mother into the car and took us to the clinic. My mom was the only one who knew I was a girl.

The clinic was the best in the city; it had lamps outside the birthing rooms to indicate if the baby was born a boy or a girl.

17

A light outside the doorway would light up blue for a boy and pink for a girl.

My siblings and extended family eagerly waited for the reveal in the waiting room as they kept a steady eye on the doorway.

My family was what you would consider an affluent, picture-perfect family. It consisted of a beautiful wife, a successful husband, and four children, who judging by their brand name clothes, looked more American than Venezuelan.

I had two brothers and two sisters. My eldest brother Robert was 16 years old when I was born. My eldest sister, Karina, was 14. My middle sister Evelyn was 11, and my youngest brother Julio was nine. We also had a half-sister who was 19 years old at the time of my birth, but my siblings and I learned about her much later.

The last trip we took as a family, I was one year old

While my family waited outside of the birthing room, my father, as a joke, told the doctor to turn on the blue light when I was born. Everyone celebrated a boy, and then the pink light came on, flashing for emphasis. Although initially confused, everyone learned and accepted that I was a girl.

I wonder if my little infant heart felt acceptance rather than excitement. There was some disappointment among my siblings. The one that was disappointed the most was my father. He wanted the blue light to come on.

Young Traveler

I was born in the city of Barquisimeto, a relatively large city located about four hours from the capital, Caracas. The airport was small, so the arrival and departure areas were the same. People would run to the second floor to wave their hellos or goodbyes. It was an open-air terrace, so depending on the occasion, you could hear the loud love declarations, good lucks, or cries.

I like to watch people in the arrival halls of airports. There is so much emotion in that small space. I love to see the old man waiting with a bouquet of flowers. The woman with small children greeting her husband as he returns from war. The mother hugging her son. I love to watch the reunions, the smiles, the tears of joy, and the love because it is all very different from most of what I experienced in airports during my early life.

I stepped onto that second-floor open terrace in Barquisimeto several times during my childhood. Still, more often than not, I was the one going to or coming from the plane. When I arrived, I would hear my sister Karina shouting my name. I used to get so excited watching the arms eagerly waving hello. When I departed, I would look back and see tears running down my sister Karina's face as she waved goodbye.

My most vivid memory of arriving at the airport is when I was five years old. And by memory, I mean that there is a photo of the occasion. That's how I know it happened.

My sister Karina was waiting with balloons. My dad and I were coming from New York. I was wearing a cute jean jumper and ponytails. My hair was long, blond, and glistened in the sun. Just a few hours before, I had hugged my mom goodbye in Brooklyn. She cried as she watched me walk away, holding my dad's hand. There were so many tears in my childhood.

My sister tells me that I ran towards her and wrapped my little arms around her neck. She was 20 years old, enrolled in the university, and had a boyfriend. However, I was the most important person in her life from the moment I was born.

Evelin, Karina, Me in Karina's arms, Julio in Barquisimeto

A Gift for My Sister

One late night, shortly after I was born, my mom went to check up on me to make sure I was sleeping okay. The crib was empty, and my mother panicked. She found me sleeping comfortably in my sister's arms. We often snuggled in her bed after she fed me an extra bottle of milk.

Karina fed me many extra bottles of milk. My mom blamed her for my excessive love of food. When I was a teen, mom would say to Karina, half laughing and half serious, "You overfed her when she was a baby; that is why she can eat a whole pizza."

My arrival into the family surprised my other siblings but more than a surprise, I was a gift for my sister. When she was a teenager, Karina dreamed about having a baby. Her desire was so strong that my mom sometimes hinted at the fact that she had me just so my sister wouldn't go and try to get a baby herself.

21

My Brother's Fate

Robert was a healthy child and appeared to be a healthy young adult. One day he was playing in the yard and hit his leg. My mom took him to a local healer to get a massage. When the man started to massage his leg, he looked at my mom and said,

"It is better you take him to the doctor."

Imaging revealed that he had a large mass in his left leg. Exams revealed it was malignant. He had sarcoma, a cancer that comes from different types of tissues.

My parents flew their 18-year-old boy to New York to get him the best care possible. They were trying to save him; cancer had other plans. By the time they arrived in New York my brother had stage IV cancer. What ensued were years of pain, grief, and broken dreams.

Some days, I played in the yard and climbed the mango trees. Other days I sat inside countless exam rooms with my mother. My mom tells me that at the beginning of this ordeal when the doctors would deliver their news about my brother's fate, I used to stretch out my little hand to hold hers.

As the months and years went by, I stopped holding her hand, and I would just watch her and everyone else from a distance. She didn't understand why that change had happened; in truth, she didn't have time to even think about it.

With my brother Robert and my mom in New York

Watching Him Die

My mother had to deal with this tragedy alone. Even when my dad was around, she was alone. My father was a successful businessman in Venezuela; he worked from morning to night.

My mom stayed in an apartment in Brooklyn during the years my brother underwent treatment, but she practically lived at the hospital. She watched her son die slowly in a city she didn't know, surrounded by people who didn't speak her language.

On top of that, she also had to deal with leaving me, her little girl, in Venezuela for months at a time. I had a very fragmented reality; I would see my mother for a week or two every three to six months. I spent the rest of the time under the care of my father, sister, aunt, and a sweet lady called Alicia.

Alicia loved to cook. She often pulled a chair beside the kitchen counter for me to stand on. I used to love dipping my little hands in a bowl of soft cornflower. I would make small balls and flatten them to look like discs. Those discs are called Arepas. They are a delicious traditional dish. I still make Arepas, and I often think of Alicia when I roll the little balls in my hands.

My brother Robert a year into his treatment

Fractured by Illness

My brother Robert spent more than two years in New York, in one of the city's finest hospitals. They kept him just barely alive. My father carried a burden on his shoulders.

24

Before my brother got sick, my father constantly shamed him for being too delicate or gay.

He never showed any love to my brother, but spent millions of dollars, his entire life's savings, trying to save him. He was likely motivated by guilt. Perhaps he wondered if all those years of constant humiliation and insults had anything to do with his son's cancer.

Robert had two sides. One side of him wanted to die even before he got sick. That part of him was constantly unhappy and in pain. He bullied my siblings relentlessly and attempted to soothe his hurt by eating full jars of mayonnaise with a spoon and fostering many unhealthy habits.

Just a few days before passing, while gasping for air, Robert angrily told my mom that the guy delivering the oxygen tank had told him,

"Just let go, be free."

The other part of him that was clinging to life was offended by the suggestion to just let go. That part wanted to be alive. A few days later, he told my mother he felt he was dying. With shortness of breath, he told her he held on just to see her one last time. His lungs gave up one December morning.

Like He Never Existed

A child who loses his or her parents is called an orphan. There is no word for parents who lose their child. Words also fall short of describing the pain that engulfs a parent who faces that tragedy. My mother still allows herself to grieve my brother's death only one day a year.

She tells me that she developed a switch. A switch much like the one in a room that turns the light on and off. She says that she turns on the light of my brother's memory only one day a year. We all develop our own coping strategies to survive tragedies; that is hers.

During a break in his treatments, Robert baked a cake with me, and my mom filmed the whole thing. I was around four years old; he was pale and so skinny you would think it was a miracle he was standing. In the video, I have flour on my nose, and I almost drop the bowl with the eggs onto the floor. I freak out and open my mouth in shock. He watches me and smiles.

I don't remember the moment; I just remember watching the video before it was disappeared, together with everything he ever owned and any photo he was on. As many families do, our family tried to erase him from our memories after his death.

The attempts at disappearing my brother's memory were successful. I grew up feeling as if he never existed. When the subject of siblings came up, he was always an afterthought.

"Oh yeah...I also had a brother who died," I would say.

Navigating Loss

During Robert's illness, I had to make sense of what was happening. I had to learn big words early. Cancer, chemotherapy, sarcoma, tumor, and illness. I had to understand that all of those words led to something called death. Somehow, I had to grasp the fact that the right thing for my mom to do was to be by my dying brother's side.

Even if it made me sad, as a child, I felt I shouldn't be angry at my mom. That would be something my sister called selfish. I also thought I should never tell anyone I blamed Robert for not having my mom with me. And after his death, I never told my mom how I felt. I didn't want to hurt her feelings; she was already crying enough. That was a lot of deductive thinking to ask from a five-year-old.

I remember a little snippet from the day he died. I ran out of the front door towards some of his friends who were arriving.

I exclaimed excitedly, with a smile on my face,

"Robert died!"

The girl that came in first stared at me and violently pushed me out of the way. I always wondered why I was happy that day. That memory bothered me. I realized not too long ago that I carried a deep sense of guilt most of my life. I felt Robert was taking my mom away. When he died, I was happy because I thought I would get my mom back. In a way, I felt it was my fault he had died.

I didn't think deeply about Robert again until 31 years after his death. I was sitting next to a small palm tree one night. The wind blew its fronds onto my face; they felt like strings of hair in front of my eyes. I remembered Robert used to grab my curls and cover my eyes with them. I used to remove them angrily with the back of my three-year-old hand. He would smile and do it again and again.

My brother had a short, pain-ridden life. Our paths only crossed for about five years. I didn't think that he had influenced me at all. As it turns out, I learned a valuable life lesson from him.

His Death Changed Me

I think of him when I listen to a song called *Saturn* by Sleeping at Last. The song is about the profound impact of someone's presence even after they have departed. The lyrics also highlight the breathtaking wonder and beauty of simply being alive.

When I was born, I had a flame inside of me that was hot and fierce. It was a small flame then; it just flickered. When my brother died, I understood that his inner fire had gone out. I owe him my zest for life. I have lived an incredibly full life thanks, in many ways, because I was exposed to the loss of a young life so early during mine.

Your Mirror

Within the pages of this book, you'll find a mirror reflecting the ups and downs of real life, a mirror that may remind you of your own journey. I'll share moments when my inner flicker almost went out, inviting you to reflect on the challenges you might have faced that threatened to dim your spirit.

But let me assure you, this isn't a tale of despair; instead, it's a testament to the resilience we all possess. It is a story of triumph and transformation.

As you delve into these heartfelt stories, you will witness how the profound life metamorphosis I underwent, catalyzed by alternative and revolutionary healing paths, have shaped my life.

Are you eager to take courageous steps toward transforming your life, reclaiming your greatness, and igniting your spirit even more? If so, this book will guide you to embrace the unknown and discover the extraordinary possibilities that await.

CHAPTER 3
Echoes of The Past

*"If we want to understand the oak, it's
back to the acorn we must go."*

– Oprah Winfrey

When people pass on their secrets and pain unchecked, they just keep handing down traits, beliefs, customs, or the lack thereof from one generation to another.

Exploring your roots holds the keys to understanding the profound influence of your family's past on your present.

Shortly after I turned 38, I found myself on a road trip to Arizona. I was hoping to get some inspiration for writing this book, so I decided to listen to Viola Davis' memoir. In her memoir, she eloquently describes her parents' early years.

My mom was right beside me in the car, and I suddenly realized I didn't know much about her life. We drove for five hours, and she shared stories about where she came from and the experiences that made her who she is. While listening to her, I started to untangle the intricate threads of my own life. Our conversation made me see myself and my place in the world in a whole new light.

"Mom, can we talk about your childhood?" I asked. She put her phone down and gave me her full attention.

"You told me before that some nights you would wet the bed, and your mom would just lay you on the cold floor as punishment, with no blankets," I said. The heaviness of the statement hung between us.

"Was your house often cold?" I asked.

"Yes," she said, "we had no heat."

That surprised me; I always assumed she had the basic comforts I grew up with.

Difficult Start

She said the world war had ended, and more recently, the Spanish Civil War had ended. The Canary Islands (where she was born) were like the armpit of Spain back then.

"We belonged to Spain but didn't belong to it, if you know what I mean," she explained.

"Did you at least have hot water in the shower?" I asked.

"What shower?" she said. "We didn't have running water. There was a communal place where my mother and grandmother would go and get buckets of water. We would shower by the kitchen sink with cups."

"What about the toilet, Mom?" I asked.

"We had no toilets! There was a place outside we would use as a bathroom.," she said.

"Like a pit with a seat?" I asked.

"No, not even; it was just an area," she told me as she looked out the window.

I was aghast; at that moment, it dawned on me that my mom, only one generation away from me, grew up in extreme poverty.

"You know, Mom, most of my friends and people I know are at least two generations from that type of poverty, and I don't think it was that extreme," I said. She just kept on looking out the window.

I grew up in a massive house with an even larger backyard. Until that day, I had no idea how different my parents' social status and ours had been. It was shocking, and I wanted to learn more.

The Whore's House

My great-grandmother was a tough, uneducated woman. My mom's household was deemed a 'whore's house' long before my mother came into existence, among other reasons, because my great-grandmother had birthed a child when she was 14 years old.

Birthing a child at that age was not unusual, but what labeled her as a whore, was that the father of the baby was an old married man. An old married man basically raped

32

my great-grandmother when she was a child with no consequences. And her daughter, my grandmother, ultimately embraced the stigmatized role of a "town's whore."

My grandmother knew how to sew and knit, so she always dressed my mom and aunt as if they belonged to a different, much better household.

My mom and aunt grew up running around stealing fruits and almonds from the neighbors. Love was neither given nor expressed by any family member. Kind words were nonexistent; they believed a loving comment would mess the child up.

Secret Inheritances

My mom carried that with her; even to this day, when my aunt compliments me, my mom remains silent.

I ask her, "What do you think, Mom?"

"Of course, I think the same, but I don't want to mess you up," she always replies.

As you grow up, you soak in how people around you talk and act without even realizing it. You receive secret inheritances of wisdom, advice, and quirks from your parents, teachers, and other important people.

My mom's lack of compliments used to bother me, but now I understand where that comes from, so I have much more compassion.

Your Echoes

Have you ever caught yourself saying or doing something that reminded you of someone from your childhood? It's amazing how those echoes from the past can resurface in your life, isn't it? Understanding where those patterns come from offers insights into your own identity and personal growth.

By recognizing your inherited behaviors, you hold the power to break free from anything that doesn't align with who you truly are. Awareness allows you to redefine yourself and create a life that reflects your authentic self.

A Child with Two Jobs

My mom has always been creative; she constantly paints the world in her mind. She is the most incredible Artist. When she was very little, she would often be found lying on the grass, watching the stars or the trees. When my grandmother would ask her what she was doing, she would reply,

"I am taking in the sights."

Sometimes, we get lucky, and she puts her world onto a canvas. The walls of my house are adorned with her colorful works of art.

Painting was not considered very useful when my mother was little. Sewing skills, on the other hand, were highly desirable. At eight years old, my mom stopped going to school and had two jobs instead: working at the local sewing shop and looking after her little sister.

My mom on the right, her little sister on the left

Abandoned Twice

When my mom was only four years old, and my aunt was one year old, my grandfather left the island to find a better life. He ended up in Venezuela. Back then, Venezuela was considered the promised land.

At the age of 12, my mom faced another significant upheaval when, eight years after my grandfather's departure, my grandmother also packed her bags and left without saying goodbye.

My grandmother reunited with my grandfather in Venezuela. Three years after my grandmother's sudden departure, my mom received a letter from her. My grandmother was pregnant and asked my mom to travel to Caracas to help when the baby was born. The prospect of reuniting with her mother after such a long absence was both daunting and heartwarming for my mom.

35

She left behind everything she knew and traveled alone when she was 15. She was so excited to see her mother again. But she only saw her father when she walked into the arrivals lounge at the Caracas airport. She didn't even remember his face well, but she remembered his eyes.

He delivered the terrible news: My grandmother had died seven days prior during childbirth, and the little boy had died too. They had mailed a letter to Spain, but it had not arrived on time. My mother ended up in a foreign country with a strange man. She doesn't talk much about those years, and those are not my stories to tell.

My maternal grandparents

New Woman of the House

My aunt finally arrived in Venezuela one year later. My grandfather didn't want them to go to school. So, my mom continued to work sewing clothes, and my aunt learned secretarial skills. My grandfather was mostly absent from their lives, just like his father had been absent from his.

My mom instantly became the woman of the house. She had to learn how to make bean soups, as her grandmother did. To this day, my mom's bean soups are legendary.

After many bean soups, my mother's beautiful cheekbones framed a young and pretty face. Her long dark hair went all the way down her back. Her body was perfect, with strong and defined legs, a tiny waist, and small round breasts.

My mom in her twenties

She loves telling the stories of how, when she walked down the street, the traffic would stop just to watch her go.

"One time, a guy in a motorcycle even crashed because he got distracted looking at me," she once told me, with a smile on her face. "He didn't get hurt," she added.

Still, for all of her beauty, my mom was too skinny by the beauty standards of that time. "You need to gain weight if you want a man," my grandfather often told her.

My mother often told me during my teenage years, "Melissa, you need to lose weight if you want a man."

Again, those echoes are more than just linguistic patterns, they carry the essence of the people who molded you.

The experiences, connections, and surroundings that shaped your parents' beliefs, values, and attitudes affects how you navigate through life, including how you raise your children and run your household.

In the next chapters, I invite you to step into my household. Your background and mine might be different, yet our experiences during childhood often shape us in similar ways. These similarities forge a profound and universal connection that binds us together.

Our shared vulnerability is a comforting reminder: you are not alone in carrying the weight of your past.

CHAPTER 4
Our Direction, Our Discipline

"We need to remember across generations that there is as much to learn as there is to teach."

– Gloria Steinem

Within the sanctuary of our homes, our parents sow seeds within us. These seeds take root and shape our emotions and thoughts. In some households, these seeds are of love and care. They blossom into beautiful flowers of warmth and affection. In others, however, they are seeds of neglect, pain, and hatred. They sprout as invasive weeds that overpower and overshadow the delicate flowers attempting to bloom alongside.

Experts say that parents can usually only love their kids as much as they, themselves, were loved by their parents. They also say that parents often love their children in the same way that they were loved. In short, parents generally repeat the patterns created by their parents.

I am so proud of my mother. She experienced little love from either parent during her childhood, yet she gave us so much love. She broke the pattern.

Searching for God

Religion saved my mom's life. And it gave us kids a north, a path to follow, during a very turbulent time.

By 27, my mom already had four kids; I came nine years later. My dad didn't help her to raise us. He was the family's breadwinner, and that was enough for her.

My mom had her first kid in the 70s. At that time, kids were commonly disciplined with physical punishment.

One day Mom went to slap my eldest brother, Robert, and he held her hand in the air. He was a tall 14-year-old and much stronger than her. That instant terrified her. He obliterated the only way she knew a child could be steered. She was afraid her kids would lose their way. So, she turned to religion and the Bible for help. She enrolled my siblings in Bible studies.

When I was born, my mom and siblings belonged to an organized religion. In the beginning, my dad was respectful of it. As time progressed, problems in their marriage grew bigger and bigger, and he blamed religion. He persecuted Karina and my mother relentlessly. He often threatened their lives.

Gun to the Chest

My father always had a gun with him. Once, he called all my siblings into the living room, and a heated argument about the religion ensued. He put his gun on my mom's chest. My siblings watched him pull the trigger. Something happened, and the gun didn't fire. That gun always fired; I am glad that day, it didn't.

Before he died, Robert called my father into his bedroom. He told him he had one last dying wish. He asked my father to allow my family to be part of that religion without any more opposition. My father agreed. My mom and siblings remained firm in their faith. And they shared their faith with me.

The Power of Faith

I learned very early that my mom's love was proportional to how active I was in the religion. So, I became a model child. I spent my childhood preaching to people door to door.

At eight years old, I was conducting bible studies on my own and giving short speeches on the stage. I remained very active in the religion until I was thirty-three.

Many of the people in this religion were incredible; they were loving and caring. I never felt as if I belonged with them, though. In their defense, I didn't feel like I belonged anywhere.

Looking back, I realize that being a part of that religion was, in many ways, a gift. God became real to me. Religion gave me stability. There is tremendous healing power in fellowship and faith. It is vital for children and adults to have some sort of community, somewhere they feel they belong.

Dirty Sex

On the flip side, I grew up afraid of sinning against God. We were told sex outside marriage was forbidden. Sexual desire or self-pleasuring was never explained; it felt like the whole thing was a deadly sin. All I heard as a child was that sex was dirty. No one ever talked to me about my vagina or a boy's penis.

No one had explained sex or sexuality to my mom, and her mom likely never got any explanation either. Generational burdens were passed along.

It's surprisingly common for parents to avoid uncomfortable discussions, which can have serious consequences. These gaps in understanding leave children susceptible to outside influences and misguided information.

Parents must recognize that sexual education goes far beyond teaching the mechanics of sex. It plays a fundamental and empowering role in helping children foster a healthy understanding of their bodies, navigate relationships with confidence, and grasp the vital importance of consent.

Just as sexual education provides a foundation for understanding your body and relationships, discipline lays the groundwork for how you handle challenges, learn from mistakes, and navigate through various situations.

43

Taking the Blame

Growing up, my mom was a rock in the middle of the storm for all of us. She was my only disciplinarian. She also used physical punishment to discipline me, just as her mom had used it to discipline her.

My mom tells me that she couldn't fall asleep at night as a child unless her mother spanked her. As bedtime approached, she would intentionally misbehave, seeking any form of physical contact from her mother, even if it meant enduring physical pain.

It is easier for children to accept that they are wrong rather than question the illusion of a perfect parent. The idea of a flawless parent seems more comforting, even if it means internalizing blame for things beyond their control. Young children will often sacrifice their self-esteem and emotional well-being to preserve the image of an infallible caregiver.

Your Discipline

Take a moment to reflect on your upbringing and how you were disciplined during your childhood. The discipline you experienced as a child likely impacted your beliefs, behaviors, and attitudes.

Think about the methods of discipline used by your parents or caregivers. Were they strict or lenient? Did they use punishment or rewards? How did you feel when you were disciplined? Understanding these experiences can offer valuable insights into the patterns that have shaped your responses to authority and your ability to handle challenges.

Consider how your own experiences and upbringing have influenced your approach to parenting if you have children of your own. Do you find yourself mirroring the methods of discipline your parents or caregivers employed, or have you consciously chosen a different path?

Contemplate the reasons behind your choices and their impact on your children's development. Are there aspects of your upbringing that you aim to preserve because they served you well, or do you seek to break free from patterns that you believe were detrimental?

Examining the intergenerational dynamics of discipline allows you to understand your own parenting style and make intentional decisions about how you want to guide and nurture the next generations.

Physical Punishment

At eight years old, I was as tall as my mom but still drank from my baby bottle. I used to go into the kitchen, make a milkshake and then pour it into my bottle; I was just a big child.

Proper behavior was defined by a very thin line in our house; I often stepped outside of that line. When my mom wanted to discipline me, I would run away. I was fast, and most of the time, she couldn't catch me.

When she would catch me and spank me, I wouldn't cry. She thought the discipline was not working because I wasn't crying. For reasons she didn't know, I was training myself not to feel anything. I was learning to become numb in order to survive.

45

She didn't know what to do with me, so she enrolled my brother Julio as a fellow disciplinarian. When I misbehaved, Julio was called in as an executioner. The prescribed method of execution was spanking. He was 18 years old when this drill started; I was nine years old. It lasted for about three years. It affected both of us in different ways.

Hand Marks Left on My Thighs

Getting spanked by a strong young man is very different than getting spanked by a mother. The beating was so intense that I could see his hand marks on my thighs when it was over. And if it was a bad one, little blisters would raise between his finger marks. This trauma is still with me; I don't enjoy spanking in any setting.

Julio had been severely mistreated by my eldest brother Robert. Julio used to tell me I was lucky he didn't do to me the things my brother Robert did to him.

He was right; I was lucky. Julio and I had a very turbulent relationship when we were growing up. I used to pray for the well-being of each of my family members every night; Julio was always last in my prayers.

Today we are very close. He is one of the most wonderful men I know. I am constantly in awe of his perseverance in life. Life has not been easy for him. Yet, he always finds a way to be well; he teaches me so much about gratitude. I am grateful to have him in my life.

With my brother Julio

A Life of Few Regrets

Alice Miller was a renowned Swiss psychologist and psychoanalyst known for her groundbreaking work on the effects of childhood trauma. In her book *The Drama of The Gifted Child*, she invites us to think about that feeling of abandonment: "Take, for example, the feeling of abandonment. Not that of the adult, who feels lonely and therefore turns to alcohol or drugs, goes to the movies, visits friends, or makes 'unnecessary' telephone calls to bridge the gap somehow. No, I mean the original feeling in the small infant, who had none of these means of distraction and whose communication, verbal or pre-verbal, did not reach the mother because his mother herself was deprived."

I felt abandoned by my mom. Abandoned physically during the years she was in New York and abandoned when I was left to be disciplined by my brother.

I didn't have a close relationship with my mother for the first 25 years of my life. It's been a privilege to have turned that ship around.

I strive to live a life of few regrets, and not treasuring the gift of my mother's existence would have been my biggest one. It's a constant exercise not to fall back into the familiar human territory of taking things, moments, and people for granted.

I have been gifted with a deeper understanding of the nature of our relationship. Our friendship has deepened as I navigate the very turbulent waters of my past.

In the next chapter, I explore further how what you go through during your early life influences your adult behaviors. I delve into my past to explore the brushstrokes that were painted onto my emotional canvas. I invite you to do the same.

Recent photo with my mom

CHAPTER 5
A Blank Canvas

*"Give me the child until he is seven
and I will show you the man."*

– Aristotle

Imagine that you are a canvas when you are born, a vast
and blank expanse awaiting the touch of a painter's brush.

Think about those who cared for you in your early years,
your parents, grandparents, or guardians. They painted the
first brushstrokes on the canvas of your heart. Through their
actions and presence, they painted the foundation of how
you perceive safety, love, and understanding. Just as a painter
blends colors to create a harmonious scene, these caregivers
blended their care and attention, or lack thereof, to set the
tone for your emotional landscape.

The early years of life, from birth to around seven, are
crucial for a child's brain development. During that time, your
brain is like a sponge soaking up everything it encounters.

Experiences, whether enriching or adverse, disrupt and
reshape your brain, affecting how you regulate emotions, form
attachments, and engage in social interactions.

The brushstrokes on your canvas also influence how you
perceive other people's canvases. Some people might evoke a
sense of warmth and familiarity. Others may trigger unease or
uncertainty within you.

Attachment Styles

Years ago, I read a book called *Attached: The New Science of Adult Attachment and How It Can Help You Find – and Keep – Love*. It is co-authored by Amir Levine, M.D., and Rachell S. F. Heller, M.A.

While reading that book, I learned that just as artists have unique styles, people possess distinct ways of relating to each other.

The three main recognized attachment styles are secure, anxious, and avoidant. These describe how you feel and act as an adult in relationships with those you care about.

The secure attachment style shows on your canvas as firm and confident brushstrokes. If you bear this attachment style, you likely experienced a nurturing upbringing. Your canvas was graced with hues of safety and warmth.

As an adult, you feel comfortable and loved in relationships. You trust the people you care about. You form relationships that resemble a serene and harmonious composition.

The second style is anxious. The brushstrokes on an anxious canvas look shaky. As a child, you might have faced uncertainty or inconsistency from caregivers, creating an emotional landscape marked by feelings of insecurity.

As an adult, you might seek reassurance, always echoing the questions imprinted on your canvas: "Am I loved?" and "Do I belong?" You might have an excessive fear of rejection or become clingy in your interactions.

The third type is avoidant. An avoidant canvas is hard to see or to understand. As a kid, you might have felt neglected or abandoned or had experiences that overwhelmed you.

As an adult, you tend to be uncomfortable with emotional intimacy and keep your distance from others. Feeling vulnerable or out of control is your biggest fear. You suppress your feelings and have difficulty expressing your needs or asking for help. You have a bubble around you that others can't get through.

While avoidant adults may have a fear of abandonment, their response to this fear is often to create emotional distance rather than seek out reassurance and closeness, as individuals with anxious attachment styles might do.

Jackson Pollock

I felt really confused when I first read *Attached*, which was years before I knew the full story of what happened in my childhood. As an adult, I displayed all of the characteristics of the avoidant and anxious attachment styles. They just flip-flopped.

This flip-flop was more evident in my interactions with men. If a man paid attention to me, the avoidant shadow would come out, and I would run as fast as a Jamaican sprinter. And when a man ignored me, the anxious shadow would chase him until I felt embarrassed and sorry for myself. It was a nightmare.

In recent years, as I dove deeper into my childhood, I understood that there is another, less common, attachment style. I went back to the book *Attached* and found this mention: "Three to five percent [of adults] fall into the fourth, less common category (combination anxious and avoidant)."

The fourth recognized attachment style is called disorganized.

Have you ever seen a painting by Jackson Pollock where colors and lines seem to be splashed and thrown onto the canvas? If you have a disorganized attachment style, your canvas looks like one of his paintings.

This attachment style explained my conflicting desires for closeness and extreme fear of loss and rejection. It also explained why I constantly flip-flopped between being clingy and pushing people away.

As the name describes, this attachment style comes from a disorganized childhood. You might have had an unstable childhood full of mixed messages and, in many cases, traumatic experiences.

As an adult, you might want to be close to someone, but at the same time, you feel scared of getting hurt or rejected. There is a push and pull between longing for connection and fearing intimacy.

What is Wrong with You?

When you display unwanted behaviors as an adult, our current medical models and society often ask you an unhealthy question: "What is wrong with you?" But there is a better way.

Dr. Bruce D. Perry is a renowned psychiatrist and neuroscientist specializing in studying child trauma and the impact of early experiences on brain development.

Oprah Winfrey is a highly influential American media executive, talk show host, actress, philanthropist, and producer. Utilizing her influential platform, she has brought attention to different forms of trauma, such as childhood abuse, domestic violence, and sexual assault. In their book, *What Happened to You?* they explain the importance of asking that better question—and seeking the answers.

They note that: "Very often, 'what happened' takes years to reveal itself. It takes courage to confront our actions, peel back the layers of trauma in our lives, and expose the raw truth of our past. But this is where healing begins."

Your Canvas

Take a moment to step back and observe the brushstrokes that make up your emotional landscape. Which attachment style do you display as an adult? Perhaps you find yourself seeking constant reassurance, fearing rejection, or struggling to express your needs.

Consider how your early interactions and experiences during childhood might have shaped those behaviors. Did you feel secure and loved, or were there moments of uncertainty and insecurity? Were there mixed messages or traumatic events that influenced your approach to relationships? Or perhaps you don't consciously remember your interactions?

When you answer questions, you add brushstrokes to your canvas; each stroke brings a new layer of insight and understanding. Just as an artist gathers different colors and learns new techniques to create a masterpiece, you collect information from books and conversations.

However, a canvas isn't just about adding more paint. Sometimes, even with all the right colors and techniques, the painting still feels incomplete. Similarly, having information might not automatically make everything clear. Your mind can have hidden drawers where complex thoughts or experiences are stored.

If you've been searching for answers but still feel adrift, please know that you're not alone. I faced moments when I had all the "colors" of information, yet I struggled to connect the dots between my past and my actions as an adult. As many people do, I believed, "I must have had a happy childhood." But there was more to my story than met the eye.

The truths that helped me connect the dots were locked behind closed doors in my mind. But eventually, I found the keys to unlock those doors, and I'm grateful I get to share that journey with you. It's a story full of ups and downs, twists and turns.

CHAPTER 6
The Charade

"Sometimes, those who excel at making money forget the true wealth that lies in nurturing meaningful relationships."

– Mahatma Gandhi

A few years ago, I attended a seminar where the coach asked: "Whose love did you crave the most as a child?"

I answered in my head, "My father's."

The coach asked a follow-up question: "Who did you need to be for your father?"

At first, I thought, "Perfect." I needed to be perfect. Then I realized I needed to be more than perfect. I needed to be like him. In fact, I needed to be him.

My Father's Mystery

The appearances my father had built and maintained for years started to crumble soon after I was born. Until then, life had led him to many places, and in each one, he added layers to the story of his life, layers that he couldn't sustain.

My dad left his Canary Islands home at the age of 12. His living conditions were even more humble than my mother's. His father fought in the Spanish Civil War, lost a leg, and ended up in a wheelchair. The horrors he saw during the war drove him to alcohol.

My father didn't talk much about his childhood. The little he shared with us depicted a very troubled early life. He told us he ran away from his house after his mother broke a wooden chair on his back during an argument; he had the scars to prove it.

Contraband Route

He hid in a Norwegian trading ship. When they found him, it was too late to turn the ship around. He was a little boy, skinny and malnourished, who only spoke Spanish. It was not uncommon for uninvited guests to be thrown overboard at that time. The captain spared my father's life and planned to drop him off when the ship returned to a Spanish port.

My father cleaned the decks, toilets, and cabins. They gave him a dictionary, and he learned Norwegian by reading the words and mimicking the sounds. He worked very hard, and over time, he must have become helpful to them because he lived on those ships for many years.

Despite the many storms he faced during those years, the ocean was his safe haven. The ships were his home, maybe the only home he ever had. While navigating the sea, he grew from a hard-working young boy into a hard-working adult.

His travels took him to Africa and the Middle East often. In those countries, women were prohibited from buying or wearing makeup or sexy lingerie. This is when his entrepreneurial spirit kicked in.

He established a contraband route between South America and the middle east. He hid lipsticks, makeup, and underwear inside the wall panels of the ship, using a rag on the tip of a screwdriver to open the panels so as not to leave any telltale marks. He sold his contraband to local businessmen at the ports.

One time, port security got tipped about contraband being on board. But my father's attention to detail with the screwdriver paid off.

"It was good I used a rag to cover the tip of the screwdriver because the police checked the walls with a magnifier glass," he told me.

They never caught him; he had this contraband route for years.

My father during his sailor years

The Ship Sank

When he was around 30 years old, the ship he worked on caught fire and sank. He was grateful he survived and decided to leave his sailor years behind.

He had saved money to follow his dream; he wanted to open a floating restaurant in Mexico, no one had ever done that, and he wanted to be the first. He had plotted out his future: he was determined to be rich.

As a young kid, my father had just enough money to buy the local newspaper. He used to buy it every day and read it from front to back without wrinkling a single page. Then he would fold it back to its original shape and resell it so he could buy the newspaper the next day again. While reading the newspaper, he learned about an up-and-coming country.

That country was called Venezuela. As destiny would have it, he passed by Venezuela on his way to Mexico. He planned to only stay there for a few days, but those plans changed one Sunday morning.

He met my mother that day at the local Spanish Pool Club in Caracas. As Bono puts it in his memoir, *Surrender: 40 Songs, One Story*: "If you are where you are meant to be, you'll meet whom you are meant to meet."

My parent's wedding day

A Child Raising Another Child

They married a couple of months after meeting, and my mother became pregnant shortly after. She tells me, "I was just a child raising another child. When your brother cried, I would join in and cry too."

My father was extremely business savvy. After meeting my mother, he accepted a job at a wholesale grocery distributor. He started carrying boxes of supplies and quickly learned the ins and outs of the business.

He came up with a revolutionary idea at the time; after his shift, he would visit the businesses to get their orders rather than wait for them to go to the store. After six months, he purchased 50% ownership of the secondary branch in the city I was eventually born in, Barquisimeto.

My father stole a lot of money from his partners and, after about five years, purchased the entire branch. Around that time, my family moved from a tiny apartment to a fully custom-built mansion on the other side of the city. That is the house they were living in when I was born.

My Father's Delusions

My parents were married for 15 years before I was born. Those years were sprinkled with happy memories. My family went on trips and had meals together.

I came to this world during a very turbulent time for my family; without any warning, everything changed. Shortly after my birth, my father became obsessed with my mother's whereabouts. He was convinced she was cheating on him.

My dad went from being my mother's greatest admirer to her worse nightmare. He dragged my entire family into his delusions. After I turned one year old, the pieces of their marriage started to hit the ground hard.

My father became emotionally imbalanced. He would regularly come into the house screaming my siblings' names so they would join him in the family room. He would sit them on a couch and talk badly about my mother for long periods. I was there too sometimes, but as so much from my childhood, I don't consciously remember those incidents.

Even though we all lived in the same house until I was nine, my dad stopped talking to my mother when I was about five. I was often caught in the middle delivering messages from my dad to my mom and vice versa. I don't have a single photo of the three of us. In short, I was born into a completely different life than my siblings were.

Finally, a Divorce

My mother had been asking my dad for a divorce for years. He refused to divorce her because he didn't want her to get any of his money. He tapped all the phones in the house and his businesses and listened to the conversations for hours. He created elaborate stories and schemes to get my mom to cheat on him. She never did.

When I turned nine years old, my mother understood what was happening. She told my father she would give up all monies if he divorced her, as long as she kept us. My dad agreed and kept all his money. He bought us a beautiful house, and we moved with my mother to a fancier city area.

CHAPTER 7
He will Love Me

*"Care about what other people think, and
you will always be their prisoner."*

– Lao Tzu

Love didn't come easily for me. I had to work hard to earn it.

I grew up like an only child since my siblings were much older. I didn't make friends in school. I never got invited to parties, and we no longer had parties at home.

I was bored often, and seeing my dad was the best part of my day. In the afternoons after school, I would sit for hours on our front doorsteps and play a game to pass the time before my father's white car entered the driveway: Red... green... white.... I tried to predict the color of the next car that would drive by the house on our busy street.

No One Else Mattered

My middle sister Evelyn and me were obsessed with my father; we idolized him. She was the apple of my father's eye until I was four years old, and then I took her place. When I was growing up, Evelyn used to say with a hint of hurt in her voice, "Melissa, you stole my dad."

Evelyn (left), my dad (middle) and me (14) (right)

I only had one need in my life: I needed to make my father love me. Throughout my childhood, my eyes were firmly fixed in the direction of my father; no one else mattered.

As I grew, so did my admiration for my dad. I didn't need to find any friends; he completed my world. By age six or seven, I learned I could earn my dad's love by working hard.

The Boy He Wanted

I was desperate to prove my usefulness and my worth. My dad would roll up his sleeves and work hard every day. I watched him and learned; it didn't take him long to notice my business skills and my drive. We became inseparable when I turned seven, so I thought my effort was paying off. I thought he was starting to love me.

63

By then, he owned the city's largest and most luxurious restaurant, multiple coffee shops, and a large plot of land in the city's industrial area, which he later developed into a gas station and a shopping center.

My father taught me to count money. He took me to buy supplies for the restaurant and the coffee shops. We used to go to a large warehouse similar to Costco. I would load boxes onto our shopping carts, which were heavy even for an adult man to carry.

My First Job

He would bring me to the businesses on the weekends, and I spent entire summers working with him. We mainly talked business, and I mostly observed him, the boss, on his turf. Making him proud became my obsession.

My dad and me (7)

When I turned seven, I asked my dad for a summer job. When I first asked him for that job, Dad thought I would not last. My shift at one of our coffee shops was eight hours long, and I worked five days a week, starting at six a.m.

He started paying me minimum wage, but after a month, he halved that because he thought it was too much money for a seven-year-old to make.

Every night we went out to dinner, he would sit at the table to read his newspaper, tell me what he wanted to eat, give me cash, and I would go buy it. I would return to the table with the food and the change. He would always let me keep the change. I saved all that change money plus my wages in a box for years. Little did I know that money would allow me to run away from death.

When is Your Shift Over, Sexy?

I loved to cook, so when I turned ten, I started to work in our restaurant, making fresh pasta and cleaning seafood. When I was 14, I worked in our gas station, pumping gas. The gas station was in an industrial area, with truck drivers being the primary customers.

My dad had an idea that, at the time, was revolutionary. He hired beautiful women to pump the gas instead of the usual men all other gas stations in the country had. The uniform fitted snuggly around the curves of the Venezuelan women's bodies. It was an absolute hit; the lines to our gas station went down several blocks for weeks until all the neighboring gas stations started to do the same. It became a country-wide phenomenon, and to this day, women pump gas in many of the gas stations in Venezuela.

One day, I finished my shift and wore my full uniform to the office. The uniform looked good on me; I was about 5' 7' and athletic. I turned around when I heard someone say, "When is your shift over sexy?" One of my dad's friends stood there with a sly smile on his face. My dad overheard the comment; that was the last day I pumped gas. I was promoted to office duty.

Competing with My Sister

When I was nine, I learned there was a second way to enter my father's heart. My middle sister Evelyn earned my dad's love with outstanding academic achievements. She was an extremely talented architecture student.

When she was going to the university, she was so passionate about her designs that we barely saw her. She spent days at a time inside her study room. Somedays, I would hear her scream, "Asistente, por favor!" Which means, "Assistant, please!" that was her way of calling me. I would run into her study, and she would give me some tasks to help her with. I loved helping her with her projects.

I saw how proud my dad was of her. He used to spend hours with her looking at her projects, and I yearned for that approval too. Up to that point, my school performance was average at best. I didn't go to a good school; I just went to the school closest to our house.

Did He Love Me?

I needed to change schools when we moved after the divorce. A new ritzy school was having aptitude tests. I wanted to be admitted there. But I failed the tests, every single one of them. It crushed me; I was deeply embarrassed.

I don't remember if my dad judged me harshly. He didn't have to. I measured myself by the strictest standards. I vowed never to experience that kind of failure again.

From that moment on, I got a perfect score on nearly every test, quiz, or project I ever did until the day I graduated college.

I don't recall if my father ever told me he loved me. It didn't matter because I loved him.

"He must love me because he walks around with his shirt pocket full of my perfect score quizzes. He drives across the city almost every night to take me to dinner. He spends the weekends with me, and during baseball season, he takes me to many games," I thought.

My mom used to say I was lucky because he spent more time with me than he ever did with all of my siblings combined. I felt special.

As a child, I accepted that my worth was derived from my worship of God, entrepreneurial skills, and academic achievements. The standard I set for myself was as tall as Mount Everest. I climbed that mountain barefoot and was unprepared for most of my life. It was exhausting.

Good Girl

As a teenager, I was the perfect daughter, intelligent, obedient to a fault, business savvy, driven, and sporty. As lovers do, my dad and I held hands when walking in the mall. I was highly protective of him. He got many smacks on the head when I caught him looking at pretty women.

My dad saw himself in me. I was a worthy adversary, as they say. But my need to be a "good girl" overtook my personality. I became a pleaser with him; I didn't want to do anything that would make him stop loving me.

When I was five years old, he tested me. It was just the two of us in the house. He sat me on his office chair and put his gun on the desk right in front of me. He said, "I am going to shower, do not touch the gun."

I sat there, and I obeyed. When he returned, he checked to see if the gun was in the exact position he had left it in. It was; I didn't touch it. He said: "Good girl."

Your Tough Questions

Have you ever wondered if the love and admiration you received as a child were truly for who you were or merely for what you achieved or pretended to be?

It's essential to delve into the impact of your childhood experiences because, when left unchecked, they shape how you view and value yourself as an adult.

You might find yourself constantly seeking validation from others or basing your self-worth on external achievements. You may be burdened by self-doubt and by the need to be perfect.

Alice Miller writes in her book *The Drama of the gifted child* that one of the turning points in therapy happens "when the patient comes to the emotional insight that all the love, she has captured with so much effort and self-denial was not meant for her as she really was, that the admiration for her beauty and achievements was aimed at this beauty and these achievements and not at the child herself. In therapy, the small and lonely child that is hidden behind her achievements wakes up and asks: What would have happened if I had appeared before you [mom or dad] sad, needy, angry, furious? Where would your love have been then? And I was all these things as well. Does this mean that it was not really me you loved, but only what I pretended to be? The well-behaved, reliable, empathic, understanding, and convenient child, who in fact was never a child at all? What became of my childhood? Have I not been cheated out of it? I can never return to it. I can never make up for it. From the beginning I have been a little adult."

I have asked these questions of my mother. It has been a painful but healing process. I never got the chance to ask them to my father.

My father

CHAPTER 8
An Uninvited Guest

"That which does not kill us makes us stronger."
- Friedrich Nietzsche

My father was the first love of my life. When I was 14 years old, he gave me a pendant with an engraving that read:

"Yo ya no tengo nada

todo lo perdí,

para dios me queda el alma

y el corazón para ti."

Loosely translated, that is:
"I don't have anything left

everything was lost,

for God I have my soul

my heart is for you."

Me (16) at the beach

When I was 16 years old, something happened that changed me forever.

I woke up at 7:00 a.m. one Saturday morning with the golden sun shining outside my window. I didn't know that sunrise was the last happy sunrise I would see for a long time.

I planned to spend that weekend with my friend Maru and her mother. We were going to a town located near the sea called Tucacas. My suitcases were ready for my two-hour car trip. The waves, sky-colored water, and sun-heated sand were waiting.

We arrived at Tucacas around mid-morning, dropped off our belongings, and took a boat to the islands. We had a wonderful time. In the early evening, we went back to my family's apartment. After dinner, I decided to call my parents to let them know I was doing well. I called my mother first, and after I talked to her, I called my father.

He said he was getting ready to go out with my brother and sister to eat and then go to the movies, something we did like clockwork every Saturday. He sounded worried; he had been worried for a few months.

My siblings and I knew he had some business problems, but he never talked about them. Our conversation was brief; I said "good night" and hung up the phone.

Shaken on My Bed

Little did I know that I'd just had my last conversation with my father; we had said our final goodnight. I don't recall waking between 1:25 and 1:30 a.m., but I must have shaken on my bed because my life changed forever during those minutes.

My friend's mom woke me up the following morning. Without any explanation, we drove back to my house in Barquisimeto in a hurry.

My mom and older sister were waiting outside the house when we arrived. I got out of the car and said, "Hi!", but there was no response. My mother's eyes were so wide they seemed ready to jump out of their sockets. My sister's eyes were without light, in a complete shadow.

They both approached me like a tiger going after its prey. My mom grabbed my arms so tightly that it hurt.

"What is wrong?" I asked, "Is it Daddy?"

"He is in the hospital," my mom said.

"NO," my sister screamed. "Something happened, something very bad has happened."

My eyes were full of tears even before my mother spoke. She looked me in the eye and said, "Your father is dead."

Millions of Bats

I don't remember what happened right after that. Maybe I do, but I don't want to remember. I remember taking steps backward, running from the nightmare, until I fell.

I just lay on our driveway floor, screaming for several short minutes. People say that time flies when you are having fun. I discovered in those minutes that time also flies when you are out of reality. Minutes fly when reality is so bad you don't want to return to it.

After some time, the short minutes ended, and the long ones started. Even though the sun was still shining in the sky, the sunbeams were not reaching me. I felt millions of bats were flying around me, obstructing the light.

Everything inside me became empty. I was alive, but I was not living. The air was still entering my lungs, and the blood was still running through my veins, but somehow my brain was not working.

My mom had a nurse waiting for me inside the house. She injected me with a tranquilizer. A little bit later, my mother was sitting on the couch, and I sat on the floor at her feet. I looked up and asked, "Now what?"

She looked scared and powerless.

"I don't know," she said.

That moment remains etched in my mind.

I didn't realize it then, but when I asked that question and saw how lost my mother looked, I took on the responsibility of caring for my family. In that instant, I, the youngest of five, a 16-year-old girl, became my father.

It was a hefty load to carry. My family never asked me to carry it. And no matter how much I did for them, I always felt I could have done more. Today, I am incredibly grateful when I get to help them in any way I can. I view it as a privilege.

Death Threats

We never got any clear answers about what transpired on the night of my father's murder. We learned that it was a revenge kill. A year before, some thugs went to rob my father at one of his coffee shops. He took out his gun and chased them. He shot one of them in the back.

My father started to receive death threats shortly after. He had received death threats many times in his life. He used to say, "those who threatened never do anything." He turned out to be wrong.

My father didn't have any security detail, and he lived in a motel room. On the night of his murder, someone waited for him to park his car in front of the room and shot him eight times, in the head and the heart.

My father was still holding the apple he was eating in his hand when they found his body.

The police stole all of my father's jewelry upon arrival. Everything except his watch. The watch I wore during my graduation speech.

Although the police knew who had done it, they didn't arrest anyone because my family refused to pay them for the arrest. We feared retaliation. This was very common in Venezuela, and sadly, it still is. I didn't care about no one getting arrested. My father was gone; who killed him didn't matter to me.

Death's Signature Fragrance

After that day, I was captured by an enemy that I had not met before. She told me her name was Death.

Death came uninvited into my life and made herself comfortable. She left behind an aroma of despair and pain, and I breathed it all in on the night of my father's wake.

Death impregnated everything around me; her signature fragrance was the formaldehyde odor emanating from my father's casket.

I sat next to my dad's open casket all night. I was fixated on the bullet hole on his cheek. Sitting there, I felt like a prisoner of war; that funeral room was my prison.

The glass on top of the casket was covered in puddles of my tears. Each tear told a story. Some tears fell because of the beautiful times we had shared. Others because of all the beautiful times he would miss. Most of them fell because all of a sudden, there was no one for me to love and no one left who loved me.

Angry at the Moon

At some point that night, I was pried away from the casket for a few minutes. I stood outside and looked up at the sky. I became angry, and looking up, I said hurtful things to the bright, full moon above. I hated nights with full moons for years after that.

It would be two decades before I talked to a full moon again. They say that you should pay attention to the moments when life appears to go in a full circle because the moment likely carries a lesson you need to expand on. As it turned out, both of those nights, when I talked to the full moon, have been the worst nights of my life.

CHAPTER 9
The Power of Resilience

"I can be changed by what happens to me. But I refuse to be reduced by it."

- Maya Angelou

History often repeats itself as the insidious patterns of past generations push into the present.

My mother left her home at 15 years old. And when I was 16, seven months after my father's death and four months after graduating high school, I got on a plane that took me away from everything and everyone I knew.

My dad had plans for me to study in the USA. I loved science, especially chemistry, so I dreamed of attending MIT. After his passing, all those plans disappeared. I was full of more pain and anger than I knew, and all I wanted to do was to run from the country that killed my father and start over somewhere.

I opened the box where I had stored the money from my jobs and finally counted it. It amounted to almost $20,000. I packed two bags and my dog, Dana, and flew to the United States for the first of our many adventures.

The Deportation Room

I was terrified as I approached the immigration officer at the airport. He saw my fear and took me to what I call the "deportation room." This is a room they take people to for secondary examinations. I sat on one of the chairs.

Some people were crying around me; others were catatonic. My doggie started to cry, and I was so nervous I just opened her kennel and gave her a tranquilizer, even though I'd already given her one before our flight.

I spent several hours in that room before they finally called my name.

"What's the purpose of your visit?" an officer asked. "School vacation," I said

"Why do you have a dog?"

"She gets really sad when I go on vacation," I replied.

He asked me many questions and kept on asking the same questions, over and over, for a long time.

He finally looked at me quizzically and stamped my entry, allowing me six months in the country. I don't think that officer imagined that it was possible for a 16-year-old girl to be moving to the USA alone. I was so desperate that if he had not allowed me to enter, I had already plotted in my head to fly directly to Spain.

I am so glad they didn't open my suitcases, as they usually do. They would have found goodbye cards from my family in them, and I would have been deported. I remember that day every time I enter the USA now. I am always grateful for my blue passport.

Most Americans don't have to think twice when they hand their passport to an officer at an entry port. I don't take handing mine for granted. I am incredibly grateful every time I do because I am entering the country I now call home. It is not a perfect country, but it is a safe country.

Dana and I while living in Florida

Walking Without Fear

The day after I arrived in the USA, I took Dana for a walk. The walking paths of Miramar, Florida. were pristine. I smiled the whole time. It was the first time in my life that I lived in a place where I could walk on the streets without fear.

Growing up in Venezuela was challenging. Robbers entered our home several times, one of which my father chased them out with gunfire. One bullet lodged in the handrail of our stairs and stayed there as a constant reminder of the danger around us.

Going to bed was scary. Any little noise would set me off. I would create a tortuous story in my head. I would vividly imagine that the robbers had entered the house. I would picture them coming up the stairs. I lived in a constant state

82

of fear. On countless nights, I covered my head with my sheet and waited for the door handle to wiggle. I waited for death to come.

I would eventually fall asleep and do it all over again the next night. To this day, I cannot sleep unless I lock the door to my bedroom.

Childhood traumas creep in when you least expect them. Writing this part of the book took me back to those scary times. One night, I was jolted awake by an intense fear, a sensation I hadn't experienced in over two decades. It overtook me, and I became that scared 11-year-old girl again. All the physical sensations I used to feel came back in a flash.

Feeling that intense fear as an adult and then realizing I was safe reminded me of how grateful I felt in my new house when I first moved to Florida as a teen. Even though I was very young and knew very little about life in my new country, I was sure it would all work out.

On a New Path

I planned to get a student visa and to enroll in university classes as soon as I got to Florida. But my father's entrepreneurial spirit ran deep in my veins, and I soon found myself on another path. It was serendipitous that I spent years working by his side. It is almost as if they happened so I could be ready for what lay ahead in my new life.

A couple of months after I arrived in Florida, my mom came.

"Melissa, all your siblings are grown; I need to be with you and take care of you," she said.

83

A part of me was relieved to have her with me. The other part knew it made my life more complex. I needed to get her a visa too. After some research, we hired an attorney who explained that if we bought a business, we could get her an investor's visa, and I would also get a visa as a dependent minor.

Venezuela has had a currency control system for decades. The Venezuelan money is as good as toilet paper in any other country. The bolivar can't be exchanged legally into any other currency.

Despite that, my father managed to convert some of the bolivares into dollars on a secondary market and to take them out of the country illegally. He left me and each of my siblings about $400,000 cash in American bank accounts. I intended to use some of my share to buy the business we needed.

Fifteen Employees

I searched for business ideas on the Internet. I decided a franchise was the best idea because they had systems. I wanted a McDonald's, but that franchise was around $1,000,000, and I didn't have that. I saw that a local Dairy Queen, a national ice cream franchise, always had a line out the door. So, I asked the owner if he would sell it to me.

He actually burst out laughing. I don't blame him; there I was, a young girl with a heavy accent, asking to buy his business. I must have said something right, because he agreed to a meeting with my sister Karina and me. We met with the man, and he decided to sell. The franchise needed to approve the transaction too. The Dairy Queen representatives flew in to meet me, and somehow, they agreed to the sale too. I bought the business under my mom's name.

I had been by my father's side as he ran his businesses for most of my life. I learned how to handle staff and incidents. I was great at counting money but I had never written a check in English. I now owned a business with 15 part-time employees, some older than me, most around my same age. And there I was, staring at a blank check, not knowing how to write it.

My mom is an artist who brings life onto canvases. She is not a businesswoman, and she doesn't speak any English. Her role in the business was to decorate the ice cream cakes every couple of days. They were beautiful. My role was everything else.

Cold as Ice Cream

I held thousands of ice cream cones in my hand during the years I owned the ice cream shop. I filled them with creamy soft serve, making two mounds and turning my hand clockwise to make the signature curl on the top. Some customers would want their cones dipped in chocolate. I would masterfully tilt the ice cream cone upside down and dip it in the dark liquid. The warm melted chocolate would swiftly harden into a shell.

During those years, I was as cold as that soft-serve ice cream. Stepping into a full-time university curriculum while also running a busy business created another hardened shell around me. Very similar to the shell on that chocolate-dipped cone.

My Sexy Accent

Experts say that if you learn a second language before you are 14 years old, you will likely sound like a native speaker.

I learned English after I was 16 years old, so I have an accent. For years, I tried to perfect it. I now accept that my accent has a mind of its own; I'm even told it is sexy. I am glad I was never able to lose it.

I had only learned basic English in high school. I was desperate to move to the USA, so I spent the entire summer after my dad died learning English. I sat for hours on my desk with lyric books from my favorite artist. Those little books that used to come with CDs. I also had an electronic mini-translator device.

I listened to a wide range of music, from boy bands like the Backstreet Boys and Westlife to the Cranberries and Red-hot chili peppers. And to English records by Latin singers such as Ricky Martin and Enrique Iglesias. I would play the music over and over. Stopping after every sentence.

Translating every word I didn't know and writing the translation in the lyrics book.

At first, the book was not large enough to fit all the words I didn't know. When the summer ended, there were only a few unknown words per page. I still remember learning the word tongue, singing one of Enrique Iglesias' songs.

Without knowing, I was learning a language out of necessity, very similarly to how my father learned Norwegian. The constant repetition and the mimicking of the sounds allowed me to become proficient in three months. When I arrived in the USA, my English was good enough to enroll in university-level classes.

Teaching Myself to Drive

I was a teenager trapped in an adult body living a grownup life. Before I left Venezuela, I'd also learned to drive. I taught myself when my mom went on a trip with my brother.

Tears ran down my cheeks when I sat in the driver's seat of my mom's car. My dad was supposed to teach me that summer. It was one of a million little things we would never do together. I put the car in reverse and I realized that it moved on its own unless I pressed the brake. And just like that, I drove off. I drove across the city and back. By the time I pulled up to our house again, I was a driver.

I faced many situations like that during my early life. Out of need, in order to survive, I was forced to develop resilience.

Resilience is a superpower that helps you when things get tough, or you face life challenges. It's like having a special shield that protects you and helps you bounce back when bad things happen.

All the circumstances I faced gave me an invaluable gift. The gift I call "past references."

Every time you conquer an obstacle, you create memories of success. When you face other challenges, you can open your treasure chest of memories and gain strength knowing that you have climbed a similar mountain before.

The memories help you believe in yourself and show you that you have the strength and skills to overcome difficulties.

Without the superpower of resilience I developed in my early life, I wouldn't have been able to survive my adulthood.

Almost Getting Deported

Living at home and in peace was one goal I could not achieve during those years in Florida. If my mom was water, I managed to become oil. We had nothing in common other than the religion. Our relationship at home was not a harmonious one.

I was 19 years old when I got more unexpected news. One day, my mother brought me an envelope.

"It looks like something important," she said.

Department of Homeland Security was stamped on the top left corner. The letter delineated how I broke the law and described the start of my removal proceedings. Alternatively, it said I had 30 days to leave the country, and all would be well.

Needless to say, I held my breath, and my pulse quickened. When I couldn't reach my immigration attorney on the phone, I drove to his office. It was empty, and a for lease sign hung on the door. My attorney had been dishonest, and without going into detail, my visa had been revoked.

Outwardly, I pretended to be devastated; inwardly, I was relieved. I wanted to run away from the life I was living. I felt imprisoned while I lived in Florida. That letter from Homeland Security gave me freedom. It was time for a new adventure. It was time to run again.

"What are You Doing Here, Luv?"

I applied to three universities, one in Australia, another in England, and the last in Ireland. I didn't want to learn chemistry again in a language other than English.

England replied first, and off I went. I landed at the Manchester airport, feeling completely scared. I had not traveled alone since I moved to the USA three years before. I got in a taxi outside the airport; it took me to my new city which was two hours away.

"What are you doing here, luv?" said my taxi driver. His thick Yorkshire accent sounded nothing like the sexy accent James Bond had in the movies.

As cheerfully as I could, I said, "I am moving here to go to the university."

"Don't you know this city was voted the worse one to live in the UK just last week?" he said.

"No, I didn't know that," I said, as dread and fear set in. I did not enjoy my time in the city of Kingston Upon Hull. It was rainy, dark, and cold, but I had music and resilience to keep me alive.

CHAPTER 10
Harmony Amidst Chaos

"Grief and resilience live together."
– Michelle Obama

The last time I saw my dad was three nights before his murder. We sat at the local Wendy's for dinner. He told me words that would come to have deep meaning.

After my father passed away, I felt lost. I didn't know how to process the overwhelming grief that consumed me. Dealing with my sadness was tough, and my family didn't know how to help.

I was unable to speak about my father's death for nearly five years. I couldn't even mention my dad's name. When I would try, my throat would completely close up. It felt like a lock on my trachea prevented me from voicing anything that had to do with my father, my grief, or his death.

The Last Conversation

On the outside, I acted as a competent young adult. I looked healthy and well put together. The truth is that I was drowning, gasping for air. I had no outlet for my grief. And then, as soon as I moved to Florida, I discovered U2. The Irish band.

Following my father's death, I listened to the song "Kite" by U2 thousands of times. On a good day, I would play it a handful of times and cry. On a bad day, I would have it on repeat for a long while and wail.

The song carries a personal and heartfelt message. Bono sings: "I want you to know, that you don't need me anymore. I want you to know, you don't need anyone or anything at all." The song then ends with thought-provoking lines: "Who's to know when the time's come around? Don't want to see you cry, I know that this is not goodbye."

The lyrics echoed the sentiment of my father's last conversation with me. In that conversation, he delved into some heavy stuff for the first time. He was worried about what would happen to me after he was gone and wanted to ensure I would keep pursuing my academic goals.

He said something that impacted me and, in a way, made me feel isolated. He told me I didn't need anyone in my life anymore, not even him.

The last words you hear from a loved one before they die carry much emotional weight. His last words encouraged me to put up more walls and to keep myself closed off from others. I felt like I had to face everything alone, and I did for most of my life.

Have you ever seen two lions fight? When the fight ends, they each go their own way and often shake their bodies. The shaking helps them release pent-up energy. They are resetting their nervous system, heart rate, and breath.

That is what U2's song "Kite," did for me. Releasing my pain while listening to this song was the only way I could cry. Listening to it became a vital cathartic experience. Shedding tears and allowing myself to emotionally "shake" was a necessary step in my healing process. It became a way to reset and regain strength, enabling me to face the day's challenges.

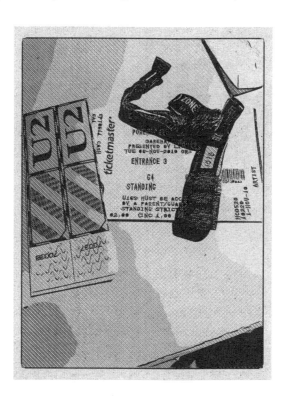

A Fantastic Universe

I still remember the first time I saw U2 live, in Boston, in 2005, a few months before I moved to England.

I was staying in a hotel next to the arena. I couldn't sleep, I was so excited. I heard voices in the middle of the night. At one point, I heard the word U2. So, I jumped out of bed and walked to the arena to see what was happening.

There were people lined up there. It was a freezing night in Boston, but I joined the line. I sat beside a sweet guy who explained the fantastic universe I was stepping into. There were line systems and fan clubs. And a lottery determined who got the front-row spots.

It was a totally unknown realm that excited me beyond belief. Being there, attending that show changed the course of my life in more ways than one.

If you won the random lottery when you scanned your ticket, an alarm would sound, and you would have the privilege of walking into the prime, coveted positions in front of the stage. As I entered, the alarm went off.

A Little Monkey

I was on the rail during the show, right in front of The Edge. I was hypnotized; all I could hear were the fantastic sounds and voices coming from the stage. Nothing around me mattered. It was just me, these four men, and their music.

For those two hours, I was the happiest I had ever been. Until that night, my life was just a dry branch with tiny flower buds, and the live music made the flowers bloom. I became a little monkey clinging onto that U2 branch. I have been holding on to it ever since.

Following U2 around the world when they toured, usually every four years, was one of the ways I kept myself alive. Their music was the only medicine I knew for the first 36 years of my life. Their songs became a lifeline, an anchor that held me steady during the darkest times.

Even though music resonated deeply within my soul, it was not enough to help me cope with the challenges that came next.

Your Lifelines

In your journey through life's trials, you have likely encountered moments when pain threatened to suffocate you.

Yet, by embracing your unique avenues for catharsis, whether through music, art, or reflection, you grant yourself the gift of emotional liberation.

Take a few moments to consider the lifelines that have supported you during challenging times. Acknowledge their significance and the role they played in your journey. They are not crutches but bridges connecting you to strength beyond measure. Seeking support, whether through friends, family, or therapeutic outlets, isn't a weakness; it's an affirmation of your humanity. It is a courageous step towards healing and growth.

CHAPTER 11
From Fortune to Folly

"Adversity introduces a man to himself."
– Albert Einstein

After a year and a half, I ran away from the English weather and moved in with my sister, Karina, in Florida. If I was the black sheep of the family, Karina was widely regarded as the golden sheep of the family. She is an extraordinary woman with a heart of gold.

Despite having the same religious background, our differing personalities led to clashes and challenges in our relationship.

Karina and I started to invest in real estate. The market was booming, so we embarked on a journey driven by the allure of quick profits. We bought houses, held them for a short period, and sold them at substantial gains. It felt like the American dream. We had no idea what we were doing.

My three siblings and I decided to invest in the same high-rise building on Brickell Avenue in downtown Miami. The developer held a launch party in Miami Beach on the rooftop of a building. I remember looking like a rock star that night. I also remember overeating and running to the bathroom to vomit during the party. Appearances are often deceiving.

The following week, everything came crashing down. It was 2008. The world's economy collapsed; we were just some of the unlucky ones who lost everything.

The Curse

My father's mother was a skinny lady with white hair. She moved to Venezuela a few years before I was born. We rarely went to her house. When we did, it was to drop off chicken bones. She was, and I know this might sound odd, a black witch. She practiced malevolent magic. For real!

She had conjured some kind of spell to ensure my father's financial success. When I was growing up, he had a large bucket on one side of his desk. My grandmother had filled it with sulfur and placed large denomination bills and coins inside. The bucket was never to be touched, and the contents didn't change over the years.

When I was seven, my father took us to say goodbye. On her deathbed, she said that we would lose all of our money seven years after my dad died. My dad made me lean over to give her a final kiss; as soon as I got near, she pounced on me and bit my ear. Blood ran down my neck. She smiled as she looked at me. That was the last time I saw her.

My siblings and I didn't think about what she said until 2008. Exactly seven years after my father's death, we had, in fact, lost it all.

A Fake Job

The next two years after losing my father's money were very hard. I stopped going to the university and lost my student visa.

Someone offered me a job in Spain. Driven by a sense of adventure and a desire to run again, I decided to uproot my life and move to Barcelona, despite never having been there.

As I settled into that vibrant city, the truth behind the job began to unravel. The promises were not upheld, leaving me disillusioned and uncertain about my future.

Forcing Myself to Vomit

At 23, I was trapped in the clutches of despair and battling bulimia. I ate incredibly large meals. Whole pizzas, 50 little sushi rolls, three hamburgers.

I tried to find solace in food, consuming enormous quantities in a desperate attempt to fill an emotional void. I forced myself to vomit for the first time when I was 21 years old. In that instant, as I knelled next to a toilet, a new coping mechanism was born—one that provided a fleeting sense of control and emotional release. The destructive cycle of binging and purging consumed my life, shrouding it in secrecy and shame.

I had learned that acids were produced in the stomach during digestion and that vomiting could destroy the esophagus and teeth. So, my system was to binge-eat and vomit before digestion.

Some days I would vomit as many as eight times. I learned to vomit very quickly and effectively. I meticulously cleaned hundreds of toilets after purging. I left no trace.

No one ever knew I struggled with bulimia for over five years. I stopped a year into my marriage. I didn't want my then-husband to be disgusted by me.

Hiding the Clues

A large number of people around the world suffer from bulimia or similar eating disorders. Anorexia, for example, is sometimes easier to identify. There is usually a significant weight loss, and the person might be obsessed with body size or might have a distorted body image view.

People who suffer from bulimia are harder to identify. It is easy to maintain an average weight while being bulimic. Just like me, they might learn techniques to hide the clues. They may use breath mints, mouthwash, or gum to mask the smell of vomit. Or have elaborate excuses to explain why they always need to go to the bathroom after eating. They might blame a fast metabolism for their constant hunger.

Externally, I showed no signs of a problem, but my body was not getting enough nutrients. I was diagnosed with anemia. I was losing my hair, had very few eyelashes, and wouldn't have my period for months at a time. Still, no one connected the dots, not even I did.

Compulsive Behaviors

Compulsive behaviors were not new to me. In my early childhood, I had constant nose bleeds. They were caused by a compulsive nose-picking disorder that lasted for a couple of years.

When I was 10, I developed another form of body-focused repetitive behavior. I compulsively touched my hair. My hair was getting damaged, so I adapted and twirled the strands near my neck instead.

Engaging in the repetitive motion distracted me and allowed me to release tension. The focus on the physical sensation and the act itself offered a brief escape from emotional discomfort.

This behavior became so ingrained that I sometimes still touch my hair in that repetitive way. My middle sister Evelyn suffered from the same compulsion for many years.

People use many other coping mechanisms to deal with emotional distress, such as self-cutting or scab picking to activate the body's natural pain response, which releases endorphins and other neurochemicals that may temporarily elevate mood and provide a sense of calm or emotional numbness.

It's common for people to develop coping mechanisms as a response to trauma or challenging life circumstances. However, it is important to note that not all compulsive or addictive behaviors are rooted in trauma. Dr. Gabor Maté is a renowned physician, speaker, and author known for his work in the field of addiction, trauma, and mind-body health. He explains it very well in his book *In the Realm of Hungry Ghosts: Close Encounters with Addiction:*

"Not all addictions are rooted in abuse or trauma, but I do believe they can all be traced to painful experiences… The wound may not be as deep and the ache not as excruciating, and it may even be entirely hidden—but it's there. As we'll see, the effects of early stress or adverse experiences directly shape both the psychology and the neurobiology of addiction in the brain."

Hidden Threads of Trauma

Recognizing and acknowledging the signs of trauma or painful experiences can be challenging, and it requires readiness and willingness to face and address those issues. Sometimes, you may be unaware of the connection between your behaviors or emotions and past traumatic experiences.

You might consciously or unconsciously ignore or suppress those signs for various reasons, such as fear, shame, guilt, or a lack of understanding about trauma and its effects.

Peter A. Levine is a renowned psychologist and trauma and somatic experiencing expert. In his book, *In an Unspoken Voice*, he explains, "When we fight against and/or hide from unpleasant or painful sensations and feelings, we generally make things worse. The more we avoid them, the greater the power they exert upon our behavior and sense of well-being. What is not felt remains the same or is intensified, generating a cascade of virulent and corrosive emotions. This forces us to fortify our methods of defense, avoidance and control. This is the vicious cycle created by trauma."

Some of my coping mechanisms started very early, while others developed later. I didn't realize that they were related. Most families are not educated on mental health issues. My family was no different. I was just told, time and time again, to stop. No one ever wondered why I had those compulsions in the first place, not even me.

I went through life trying to avoid my uncomfortable emotions. However, those years lost to pain were not wasted; they were an integral part of my journey.

Your Unique Self

Have you kept some of your challenges a secret? Perhaps because mental health wasn't openly discussed or understood in your family? Or maybe you equated your self-worth with external achievements or appearances? The weight of these unspoken struggles might have led you to isolate yourself, creating a facade of strength while battling your own demons behind closed doors.

Don't shy away from asking the uncomfortable questions. Those inquiries allow you to better understand yourself and to demystify the patterns influencing your life. The answers to your questions are crucial for your growth.

Think about how sharing your struggles with someone you trust could lead to a deeper connection and a sense of liberation. It's not an admission of defeat but rather a courageous step towards self-discovery and healing.

By embracing your imperfections, you empower others to do the same, fostering an environment of empathy and understanding. After all, when we allow ourselves to be authentically seen, we give permission to those around us to do the same, breaking the cycle of silence that perpetuates unnecessary suffering.

CHAPTER 12
A Desperate Union

*"The right way to wholeness is made up of
fateful detours and wrong turnings."*

– C.G.Jung

We all have a deep-rooted need to love and be loved;
nothing in the world can replace it. I didn't want love to be
the appendix of my life's book. I wanted my whole book to be
about love.

I had many little boyfriends when I was young, but my
teens and early 20s were loveless.

Our religion had big conventions several times a year.
I would buy new clothes, blow dry my hair, and get my nails
done. I would wear uncomfortable heels and walk around the
venue during all the breaks, waiting for prince charming to
show up. I cried on my way home countless times because he
never did.

My family would try to console me telling me that the
guys were just intimidated by me. That was not what a young
girl wanted to hear. A part of me knew they were right,
though. I overwhelmed the boys.

I was responsible, business savvy, and mature. Twenty-
year-old boys are not looking for that. I am proud of myself
because I didn't change who I was just to make a guy more
comfortable. It left me lonely, and it definitely affected my
self-worth.

A Real Man

When I was 21 years old, I met an older man. He was not overwhelmed by me; I thought he was a real man. He was the most handsome guy I had ever seen. He was so interesting, popular, and sweet. I was shocked when he paid attention to me. It was fun to dream of him.

During this short-lived connection, I experienced a newfound sense of self-worth. Even though our encounters were only sexual, feeling that someone like him desired me made me feel special.

Although nothing tangible came out of it, I was very grateful for the brief times we spent together because at least I felt pretty, for the first time ever.

Being intimate with him created questions in my mind. Questions I didn't care to answer for many years.

Working at McDonald's

Three years passed, and right after I turned 25, I married the next guy who told me I was pretty. I met him thanks to a U2 tour.

My self-pity had me sitting on my couch for nearly a year in Barcelona. Then U2 announced a tour that would start in two months at a stadium 15 min from where I lived. I calculated I needed to make at least $18,000 to follow them around the world for a couple of months.

I looked for jobs and quickly realized that the hiring process in Spain could take months. So, I joined about 300 people in interviews for the one place that would hire fast, McDonald's.

A bachelor's degree was required for any managerial position, but I had only finished my two-year degree. And due to my professional experience, I was overqualified for anything else. I didn't care; I took the position they offered me.

I worked 16 hours per day taking customers' orders. I volunteered for all the overtime shifts and went to the gym during the one-hour lunch break.

I remember walking back to my apartment at 2 a.m. every night while devouring a bag full of hamburgers and several cups of ice cream. Once in my apartment, I would kneel next to my toilet and feel sorry for myself before I purged and went to bed.

Those two months were exhausting. However, all the effort was worth it because I enjoyed many beautiful concerts and changed the direction of my life. The path that unfolded in the years that followed was fraught with challenges, testing my resilience at every turn. But that very path ultimately brought me to where I stand today.

If you're currently navigating a complex and uncertain journey, one that is pushing your limits and has you questioning your desire to be alive, I want you to know that I've been there too. In those moments of doubt and fatigue, holding onto your courage is crucial.

The hours before sunrise are the darkest and coldest. Soon thereafter, the world is bathed in light and warmth. The most challenging and turbulent times often occur just before a significant positive change or breakthrough. So, hang in there; better times could be just around the corner.

A Life-Altering Cruise

My U2 travels took me back to the USA, where I met the man who would become my husband. He was widely traveled, European, ten years older, and belonged to the same religion.

I was physically attracted to a couple of young guys growing up and chased them. They never cared about chasing me back. Although this guy was handsome, he was not really my type, so it was easy for me not to chase him. Not being chased by a woman was new to him, and it attracted him.

I recall the weight of my insecurities pressing upon me, casting a shadow over my self-worth. I was grappling with many challenges, feeling lost and uncertain about my future. During this emotional turmoil, he appeared to offer stability and security. I thought he could be an anchor in the tempestuous sea of my life.

We met online and started to date. We only spent two weeks together before I traveled back to Spain. We had been long-distance dating for about a month when I decided to go on a cruise around the Mediterranean with my family. I was shocked when this man jumped out from behind a bush as we entered the ship; no one in my family knew he planned on joining the cruise.

I had a lot of mixed emotions. A part of me was happy he was there; the other part was scared. Dating someone intimidated me.

A week into the cruise, we stopped in Greece. The city of Athens is beautiful. There is a rocky hill with ancient ruins on top. The ruins are called the Acropolis. The most famous Greek temple is there. It is called the Parthenon. I was walking by that temple when this guy knelt down in front of me and asked: "Will you marry me?"

He proposed less than two months after we met.

I had dreamed about the day the man of my dreams asked me to marry him. As I looked at the ring and him, my gut said something. I didn't listen. Instead, I said, "Yes."

Marriage proposal in front of the Parthenon

Not the Dream Wedding

Our brief courtship was a whirlwind of conflicting emotions. On the one hand, I yearned for love and a genuine connection, yet on the other, I battled the nagging doubts and fears that consumed my thoughts. It was in this vulnerable state that I decided to tie the knot.

I had broken the "no sex before marriage rule" a couple of times by then. But I didn't have sex with my fiancé until our wedding day. I wanted to start our marriage on the right foot.

We were legally married outside of Charleston, South Carolina, on the grass in front of the town hall. We went to have lunch at Carrabba's afterward. It was a very dark day for me.

Misguided Hope

I had been convincing myself to marry this guy because I always thought I would be in love when I married. We barely knew each other. There was infatuation, and I was excited about the new life. But there was no deep love on either side.

History again repeated itself. Just like my mom, I entered a marriage with the misguided hope that love would eventually blossom.

My family did not ask any questions. They wanted me to stop traveling and living out of suitcases. They wanted me to fit in the housewife mold.

I had a habit of running that stem from being unable to run away from my childhood. I had run from Venezuela, my ice cream store, England, and Florida. But I was determined not to run away from this marriage. I didn't know much about relationships. This was my first real relationship. I wanted him to love me. And I wanted to love him.

I remember sitting on the plane on our way to our honeymoon. I leaned on his chest and put my face on his neck. I smelled his skin, and I felt butterflies in my belly. I wondered if that was how love felt.

CHAPTER 13
Emotional Bankruptcy

"Money can't buy happiness, but it can make you awfully comfortable while you're being miserable."

-Clare Boothe Luce

As a couple, my ex-husband and I were good at one thing and one thing only. Making money.

From the moment we returned from the honeymoon, I began working in the small chiropractic clinic he had near Charleston, South Carolina.

Even though my ex-husband was a doctor, he was more interested in real estate than treating patients. He had read a book called *Rich Dad, Poor Dad*. A personal finance and self-help book by Robert Kiyosaki.

The book delves into the lessons he learned from his "poor dad" (biological father) and "rich dad" (best friend's father), showcasing how their mindsets and financial education shaped their lives differently. Kiyosaki highlights the value of financial literacy, redefines notions about money and wealth, and covers key concepts like assets, liabilities, passive income, and income-generating assets.

Embracing Financial Wisdom

A year into our marriage, despite my dark history with real estate investments, I decided to also read the book. That book encouraged me to adopt a different mindset toward money, investing, and building wealth. It offered me practical advice on developing financial intelligence, making wise investment decisions, and working towards achieving financial independence.

We decided to take our clinic in a different direction. One that was revolutionary at the time. We attended many medical coaching seminars and developed a medical model that integrated many modalities under one roof.

I went to hundreds of events and fairs to attract new patients. In less than two years, we built a state-of-the-art facility with more than 25 employees and many medical providers.

Following Kiyosaki's advice, we used the profits from our medical business to venture into real estate investment. That decision helped us transform our lives.

We immersed ourselves in the world of real estate and attended numerous seminars. We began investing in small houses to familiarize ourselves with the intricacies of the market and gradually build our confidence as real estate investors.

With time, our portfolio expanded, and we set our sights on larger opportunities such as apartment complexes and mobile home parks.

Whether venturing into entrepreneurship, investing in real estate, pursuing a passion project, or seeking alternative income streams, don't hesitate to step outside the conventional boundaries. Open your mind to new avenues that can lead you toward financial independence and abundance.

However, as you will see next, financial abundance without love or purpose often leads to emotional bankruptcy.

In New Zealand with my ex-husband

Living a Fake Life

The combined income from our medical business and flourishing real estate investments propelled us into a financial prosperity we had never imagined.

At the start of our marriage, we could only afford budget accommodations like La Quinta Inn for our vacations; two years in, we could indulge in the finest luxuries life had to offer.

My love for traveling and adventure is at the core of who I am. First-class flights and stays in luxurious hotels became the norm, as we often embarked on trips that took us to breathtaking destinations worldwide.

In the early days of our marriage, I desperately clung to the hope that affection would gradually take root within me. I believed that committing myself to this man could shape my happiness and improve our relationship's dynamics.

But as time passed, I realized that love cannot be forced or fabricated. It must blossom naturally, nurtured by genuine emotions and shared experiences. Our love didn't grow because the soil of our hearts was not fertile, and we did not nurture those initial seeds of infatuation and hope.

We fought constantly, regularly shouting at each other in private and in public. The conflicts and disagreements became all-encompassing.

The constant clash of opposing viewpoints, values, and standards and the inability to find common ground took a toll on our emotional well-being. Our interactions lacked the warmth and intimacy I had always associated with love, leaving me emotionally adrift and disconnected. I yearned for the passion and depth that eluded us, and my heart grew heavy over time.

We lived two lives, as so many couples do. In our public life, we were a gorgeous couple that seemed to love each other and jetted across the world. That life was all over my Instagram.

Our private life—the real life--the one behind closed doors, was filled with unmet wants and broken dreams. Couples often keep this second life a secret. We did.

There were some good episodes here and there, but they dissipated as the years went on.

It became clear that material abundance alone cannot fulfill the deepest longings of the human spirit. True happiness and fulfillment lie not solely in financial achievements but in nurturing meaningful relationships, personal growth, and finding purpose beyond material wealth.

In Paris with my ex-husband

In a Dark Cave

One of the deepest voids in my married life was sexual. I never, not once, in eight years of marriage, experienced a deep intimate connection with my partner. Just like my mother, I was trapped in a loveless marriage.

The absence of a fulfilling sexual connection cast a dark shadow over our relationship. I felt broken and even more emotionally isolated than before I entered the marriage.

Societal expectations and religious beliefs were frequently cited, so I engaged in what felt like obligatory "quickies" solely to please my husband and fulfill my scriptural wife role. Sex was like a small wave that came ashore fast and just as swiftly retreated to the ocean without leaving a trace.

We were drowning our disappointment, anger, doubts, and pain by drinking expensive bottles of red wine in beautiful hotels. Our dark cave was lined with luxurious blankets.

I often looked at myself in the mirror and noted that my eyes were hollow, empty, and sad. They were similar to the eyes I saw in the mirror after my father died.

During all the years prior, even during hard times, something inside me told me that life would be good. I lost that spark, that hope, during the years I was married. I felt trapped because I truly loved God and wanted to do what I believed was right. Divorce was a sin, and I didn't want to sin against God.

For years, I sat on balconies overlooking lakes, mountains, and rivers, reminding myself of all the reasons I had to be happy. All of them were money or success related. "I can come to this beautiful place," or "I can help my family monetarily," or "My Dad would be proud," or "We live in a gorgeous house." After some time, those reasons stopped being enough to make life worth living.

Sitting on a balcony in Santorini, Greece

Self-fulfilling Prophecies

The weight of inadequacy settled upon me, casting a shadow over my role as a wife and woman. Unknowingly I was writing the story of my present and future from narratives based on the past. This is eloquently explained by Dr. Maté in his book *The Realm of Hungry Ghosts: Close Encounters with Addiction:*

"The greatest damage done by neglect, trauma or emotional loss is not the immediate pain they inflict but the long-term distortions they induce in the way a developing child will continue to interpret the world and her situation in it. All too often these ill-conditioned implicit beliefs become self-fulfilling prophecies in our lives. We create meanings from our unconscious interpretation of early events, and then we forge our present experiences from the meaning we've created. Unwittingly, we write the story of our future from narratives based on the past...Mindful awareness can bring into consciousness those hidden, past-based perspectives so that they no longer frame our worldview."

Daddy Issues

As our relationship unfolded, I experienced a wave of emotions that made me increasingly insecure and jealous. I yearned to feel wanted, rooted, and taken care of, but these fundamental desires were left unfulfilled.

I perpetuated a cycle that had plagued my family for generations: A cycle of loveless marriages and broken homes. I was married to a version of my father, a shrewd entrepreneur who did not prioritize me or our marriage.

I wandered through a dense forest for years, where the trees whispered sad stories and the roots whispered pain. In the next chapter, I stand at the edge of that dense forest and finally walk out.

Your Crossroads

When you stand at a crossroads on your journey, remember that you can redefine your path. What if you could break free from the chains of inherited patterns and create a new legacy for yourself and future generations? What if you could rewrite the narrative of your relationships and discover a love that honors your true worth? What story will you write for yourself? What legacy will you leave behind? The choice is yours.

CHAPTER 14
The Domino Effect

"It is such a great moment of liberation when you learn to forgive yourself, let the burden go, and walk out into a new path of promise and possibility."

– John O'Donohue

I believed that children didn't belong with adults. I was always unhappy in my marriage, especially when little Miles, my ex-husband's child, was around.

Consciously, I knew how terrible that feeling was, but I couldn't help it. I felt so powerless.

My ex-husband had 50% custody of his son. When we got married, Miles was four years old. My ex-husband was a good father. The days we had Miles were incredibly challenging for me.

I had never been around children. Mostly because I didn't like them. My ex-husband and I talked about it before we got married. I wanted stability, and he wanted a pretty girl, so we both compromised and ignored that conversation.

Unable to Love the Child

Miles was the most amazing kid I have met; smart, kind, and obedient. If I had opened my heart, he would have grabbed it like a bouquet, and we would have bloomed.

I was angry at myself because I felt I had made choices I shouldn't have made. The burden of self-blame pressed heavily on my heart, mainly due to my inability to genuinely love Miles.

On the one hand, there were valid reasons for not loving Miles' father, but on the other, I wrestled with the guilt of withholding love from an innocent child.

That was unforgivable, and it just added one more page to my already chaotic mental list of what was wrong with me. "No maternal instinct, another reason why she is broken" was the title at the top of that page.

If Miles entered through one door, in all his five-year-old cuteness, I left through the other. I would experience physical pain when forced to do things with him.

I used to tell my ex-husband that if he treated me better, I would want to be around them more. Given my current knowledge, I cannot be sure about the extent of my involvement in Miles' life, even if my relationship with my ex-husband had been better.

While my ex-husband's treatment influenced the situation, I realize that certain beliefs I held about children were not rational.

Instead of asking questions, we often develop stories to explain our puzzling behaviors. I never asked myself why I disliked children. Or why I couldn't love this little boy. Or why I had no desire to have children of my own.

With Dana and Miles (6)

Your Own Questions

Questioning yourself is not always an immediate reflex. Like many others, it's perfectly okay if you haven't delved into the depths of your emotions just yet. We all have our timelines, hesitations, and moments of uncertainty. Embrace your own pace and be gentle with yourself. When you are ready, ask the questions that burden your mind and seek the answers relentlessly.

From Erosion to Collapse

After seven years of marriage, we attended a dinner party in Switzerland, where a humiliating experience occurred. This incident marked the beginning of a domino effect that ultimately led to the end of our marriage.

While I had experienced previous episodes of pain and humiliation, this particular event proved to be the last straw. It was not solely about the severity of the humiliation but rather about the combination of all the cracks in our relationship that had been building over time, deepening into a canyon as wide as the Grand Canyon.

As a single tear trickled down my face, a profound clarity emerged that night in Switzerland; I knew deep within that I had reached a limit. But I was afraid of change.

Controlling Nature

It is hard to make peace with our choices and just move on. After that incident, I stayed in the marriage for another year because I was promised changes would happen.

Fear overshadowed my decision-making process. I was afraid of potentially losing what I believed to be God's blessing by breaking the sanctity of my marriage.

This fear was further compounded by concerns about the financial implications of a divorce. Uncertainty loomed over my future, and the unknowns cast a veil of doubt and apprehension over my choices.

The following year, I did something really desperate. I ignored my feelings, wants, and the fragile state of our marriage. Driven by external pressures and a desire to maintain the illusion of a perfect life, I agreed to undergo IVF treatment.

My ex-husband and I thought we were king and queen of the world, so we didn't just want to get pregnant. We had never tried to get pregnant naturally, instead we tried to control nature. We wanted twins, a boy and a girl. A clinic in LA helps couples with that kind of wish.

I underwent IVF treatments. My ovaries responded excessively well to the fertility medications during my first treatment. It became dangerous, so we had to pause it. During the second treatment, the opposite happened; there was a poor ovarian response. I still underwent the painful egg collection procedure, but no viable eggs were collected.

I firmly believe God intervened. Bringing a child voluntarily into a faulty marriage would have been extremely selfish and irresponsible. It would have perpetuated the cycle of broken relationships and subjected another innocent child to the consequences of our strained partnership.

The best decision of my life was not to try that again. Most women would have been shattered. Rather than feeling devastated by the failure of the fertility treatments, I experienced a sense of relief and gratitude.

Buried in Quicksand

I didn't see a way out of my marriage. Two months after the IVF procedure, I sat on a plane with tears streaming down my face. I felt life was passing me by. I was fading away, feeling the years fall on me like bricks that were burying me slowly in a quicksand of what-ifs.

And then, after we landed on the beautiful island of Mykonos, a door that should have remained closed was opened, as my then-husband violated my physical boundaries.

It was a profound betrayal, causing me to finally reach a breaking point. As I stood up from bed, I said the truest words I ever told him: "You will never touch me again." And he never has.

That night I reclined on the edge of the bed, but sleep didn't come; instead, my mind worked overtime. I looked at my life from as many angles as I could. I realized that the person I needed to forgive the most was myself.

I acknowledged the immense challenges I faced and understood I had made choices based on the information and resources available to me.

I accepted all my mistakes. The hasty marriage. The things I could have done better. The expectations I didn't meet as a stepmom and as a woman. Owning my shortcomings was the first step toward my self-absolution.

I turned off the negative chatter and realized marriage is not a death sentence. I talked to God, and I felt he understood that my soul's survival and longevity of my spirit took priority.

Covered in Blood

My complex emotions were like a never-ending succession of jab/cross punches. I hit the floor, covered in the blood of my own suffering. I could feel the referee smack the ring canvas after I fell down. He didn't count to 10 to declare my defeat. Instead, every time he hit the canvas, I could hear him scream: fear, despair, anger, disappointment, humiliation, betrayal, sadness, helplessness, defeat. I knew his last word would be death. I stood up before the count ended. I was not done; I still had too much life running through my veins.

The following day, I boarded a plane at the Athens airport to return to the USA. My life went full circle: I left this man in the same city where he proposed.

Sitting in that airport, I knew nothing about the rollercoaster ride ahead. I didn't know the journey I was embarking on would be filled with unexpected ups and downs, hurdles, and eye-opening moments.

Your Narrative

If you are entangled in a web of insecurities and fears like I used to be, be vigilant and mindful of the narratives shaping your choices and actions. When needed, break free from the limitations of your history and create a new story that empowers you to forge deeper connections, build loving homes, and nurture relationships that enrich your soul.

Your journey may be challenging, with twists and turns that surprise you, but know that each step you take toward liberation is worth it.

CHAPTER 15
Wake Up Dead Woman

"Music can change the world because
it can change people."

– Bono

Music has the power to heal the soul. Even when humanity can agree on very little, we all can enjoy music. It creates invisible strings between people who don't know each other, so in a way, it weaves us all onto collective music sheets that elevate the energy of the planet.

Timing was on my side, and U2 was on tour at the same time I decided to leave my ex-husband. U2's tours and my life's lows have always happened simultaneously.

Instead of flying straight from Athens to Charleston to sort out my mess, I decided to escape reality, as I often did, singing "Where the Streets Have No Name" and "Vertigo" at the top of my lungs.

The flight to New York was incredibly turbulent. While sitting on the plane, I wondered if I had lost my mind at some point during the years prior.

I was 33 years old and had been following this band around the world for 15 years. That pattern didn't fit my modus operandi. I was generally very rational, and this behavior was, by most accounts, irrational.

But why did I need to be rational or explain anything to anyone? I smiled and thought, "If this plane goes down and this is my end, I died being true to myself."

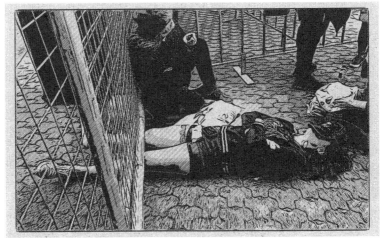

Resting outside an arena waiting for the gates to open

Sleeping on Cardboard Boxes

I arrived in the city late at night and went straight to Madison Square Garden. That arena is one of the world's most famous and historic venues. I took my place in line, sat on the cold ground, and looked back on my life.

This time I focused on my adventures following this band. How many cement floors had I sat on looking for the high of love in music? How many cold nights and hot days had I spent in foreign cities and countries, only to hear my heart beat louder?

131

Music can awaken our individual minds. That is precisely why sleeping on cardboard boxes to get an up close and personal prescription of this magical elixir was always more than a passion for me; it was a necessity.

Your Magical Potions

Just as music served as my elixir, I invite you to think about the catalysts in your life—those experiences, passions, or moments that have impacted you profoundly. They are your elixirs, your magical potions. Do more of what reconnect you with the essence of who you are and what truly matters to you.

Licking Every Drop

We all strive to master the balance between living fully in the present and having a compelling future to look forward to. As I waited at Madison Square Garden, my inner flicker reappeared; I whispered to myself *Everything will be just fine.*

Those simple words held the profound weight of faith and resilience. They encapsulated my deep-rooted trust in the universe and its inherent wisdom. No matter the obstacles that lay ahead, I knew that my dreams would guide me.

Once I left my marriage, I had the will to live again. I decided to grab onto my life as a child grabs an ice cream cone. From that moment on, I decided to lick every sticky drop that melted onto my fingers. So that, when there was no more life to live and I placed the last bit of ice cream cone in my mouth, I had few regrets and a full belly.

Regardless of how bad my marriage was, I never looked for love anywhere else. In New York, I looked straight into a man's eyes. I tilted my head, smiled, and mouthed a silent "Hi." He replied with a similar gesture and a "Hello."

The Atacama Desert is one of the driest places on Earth. Some areas haven't seen a drop of rain in more than 500 years. My heart was just like the Atacama Desert. It had been dry for at least that long. And this stranger's attention felt like dew drops falling on me, penetrating me to my core.

My heart and body absorbed it like the arid land soaks up rain when it finally comes. Almost overnight, I felt the seeds blooming. And the usually very dry Atacama turned into a beautiful carpet of flowers. I was grateful to him because I felt something.

I had no expectations of a relationship with him; we lived worlds apart, literally. Our lives were completely different, and my life was going up in flames. Yet, none of that mattered. When he didn't call, I felt totally dejected.

Life is full of unexpected encounters and unforeseen twists. We often cross paths with individuals who come into our lives to shake us awake.

Meeting this man triggered one of my deepest fears, rejection. Meeting him, however briefly, forced me to ask questions.

An 18-Wheeler Ran Me Over

As I went through my days juggling everything involved in a messy divorce, I couldn't understand why I felt like an 18-wheeler ran over me seven times just because a man I barely knew didn't show more interest in me.

It was astonishing that all the negative feelings I was experiencing in that shaky stage of my life had nothing to do with my divorce looming on the horizon and everything to do with feeling unwanted.

Determined to confront this internal turmoil, I embarked on a journey I had long contemplated, a journey of self-exploration and understanding. It was the first step towards unraveling the mysteries of my own being, a step towards discovering what lay beneath the surface.

Break Free from Your Shackles

In your quest for a fulfilling life, are you staying watchful and open to the lessons that pop up unexpectedly? Think about those times when you've met someone that impacted you? Could those surprise meetings be life's way of shaking you out of your routine?

Have you noticed those conversations that stick with you, the ones that make you think? Could they be nuggets of wisdom meant to nudge you into paying more attention to your journey?

The next time life throws you a curveball or introduces you to a new person, consider it an invitation to wake up and explore. How will you respond? Will you embrace the surprises and let them guide you to a more meaningful life? Or will you stay asleep?

Embarking on a journey of self-exploration requires courage and a willingness to face the unknown. Just as I did, you can choose to confront the hidden aspects of yourself that have been shaping your thoughts and actions. It's an adventure that may take you through the dark alleys of your past and through the sunlit fields of your dreams. Trust me, it's worth every step.

During my journey of self-discovery, I realized that the human mind is a vast and intricate landscape woven with memories, experiences, and emotions. I encountered parts of myself that I had kept locked away, and I learned to accept them with empathy and compassion.

You might encounter resistance, doubt, and fear in your journey. Your brain might be trying to protect you by keeping certain truths hidden. However, you must be resolute in your pursuit of understanding yourself fully. Break free from the shackles of self-doubt and embrace the discomfort, for it is within these challenges that the most profound growth occurs.

CHAPTER 16
The 007 of Assassins

*"Don't let your past dictate who you are, but
let it be part of who you will become."*

– Nelson Mandela

I had been dancing around attending a Tony Robbins
seminar for years. About a month after arriving from New
York, I finally booked it and went.

Tony Robbins is a well-known motivational speaker, life
coach, and author. This particular seminar was called *Unleash
the Power Within*. During the *UPW* event, participants engage
in various activities, exercises, and interactive experiences to
break through limitations, transform their mindset, and create
lasting change.

Those four days profoundly changed my life. I got to that
arena every morning wearing clean clothes and shoes, and I
left barefoot and slightly bruised every night. I was asked to
dig deep into my soul. I had never done that. At best, I had
surfed the waves of my emotions with self-help books and
YouTube videos. I was totally unprepared and shovel-less, so
I used my nails and carved into the ground that covered my
hardened heart until my fingers bled.

Those days became some of the most emotionally tooling
and physically demanding I had ever experienced. I gave it all I
had and all I didn't know I had. At times life calls you to do the
same.

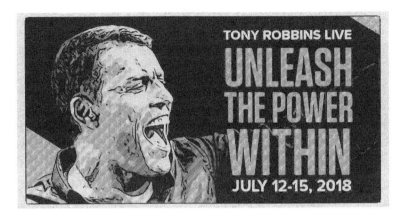

Three Ghosts

That weekend, I learned about The Dickens Process. The Dickens Process is a technique used in Neuro-Linguistic Programming (NLP) that involves exploring and transforming negative emotions or limiting beliefs. It is based on Charles Dickens' popular story, *A Christmas Carol.*

In that story, Ebenezer Scrooge is a miserable man. On Christmas morning, he faces three ghosts that give him glimpses of his past, present, and future. They show him how his life will go if he doesn't change. The future looks so bleak that he decides to change his life forever.

Our process in that seminar focused on transforming our limiting beliefs. Limiting beliefs are core beliefs you carry in your subconscious psyche. Those beliefs go unchallenged by your rational mind for most of your life. Imagine you carry beliefs you formed as a kid at perhaps two, five, or seven years old, all through your adult life and, at times, right into your grave.

Your Barriers

These beliefs create a sense of limitation and often lead to self-sabotaging behaviors. They act as barriers that prevent you from reaching your goals, pursuing your dreams, and embracing your true potential.

Here are some common examples of limiting beliefs and the consequences they carry. Do any of them apply to you?

1. **I'm not good enough:** Feeling inadequate or unworthy hinders your success in relationships, career, and personal pursuits.

2. **I don't deserve happiness/success:** Believing you're undeserving of positive outcomes sabotages your efforts to achieve happiness and fulfillment.

3. **I'm too old/young:** Age-related beliefs limit your opportunities and personal growth at different stages of life.

4. **I'm not smart/talented enough:** Underestimating your abilities prevents you from pursuing your passions and reaching your potential.

5. **Money is the root of all evil:** Associating money with negative values hinders your financial growth and abundance.

6. **I'll never find love:** Believing you are unlovable affects relationships and prevents you from forming meaningful connections.

7. **Change is too hard:** Resisting change due to fear or comfort impedes your personal development and growth.

8. **I can't trust others:** Difficulty trusting others keeps you from building strong relationships and connections.

9. **I'm a victim of circumstances:** Seeing yourself as powerless to external circumstances prevents you from taking control of your life.

10. **I am not lucky:** Believing that success solely depends on luck discourages you from putting in the necessary effort to achieve your goals.

Becoming Sherlock Holmes

Tony spent hours helping us pinpoint the three main limiting beliefs each of us carried. An incredible task in a crowd of more than 12,000. That night I became a detective;

I was like Sherlock Holmes, attempting to solve the complex mysteries of my heart.

During those hours, I felt and heard the collective cry of what seemed to be the entire human race. There were screams and wails. Tears and sadness emanated from all those strangers in that dark.

Much like the miserable man from Charles Dickens' story, we visualized our futures exactly as they would be if we continued going down the path we were walking, holding on to the same old beliefs.

That path for me was the same lonely, loveless, and sad dirt road I already knew. I didn't cry often, but I was surprised by the force of my tears that night. I was crying and screaming just like the rest because my future looked bleak.

The Blind Potter

A very valuable part of the process is that once you identify the beliefs, you work through them. Imagine you spend your whole life molding your beliefs into a piece of pottery with your eyes closed. You infuse it with your innermost fears and polish its edges with pain. You bake it over and over again until it seems unbreakable.

During The Dickens Process, you look at the pottery with your eyes open for the first time. You become the observer of this piece that has been in your hands for years, and you start to find cracks and imperfections. The more you look at it, the more you realize it's a defective piece, and you have been treasuring it as if it is a masterpiece.

Exploring your beliefs is like solving a tricky puzzle. Your thoughts run deep, so pulling them out without help can be challenging. Remember, it's okay to ask for assistance. Just like tackling a puzzle is easier with friends, seeking guidance from others can give you new insights and make the journey easier.

Men are Incapable of Love

The Dickens process was so effective that I don't even remember my second and third limiting beliefs. I do remember what my first and most prevalent limiting belief was.

I often felt rejected by boys during my teenage years, and I felt unloved during my marriage. I believed men were incapable of love and thus couldn't love me. This limiting belief was the 007 of assassins. It crept into my innermost thoughts and into my subconscious mind like a professional spy.

When I really examined that piece of pottery, something that shocked me came up. A certainty that I had never felt before washed over me. I was sure that my father had rejected me. I couldn't shake it or understand it. There was no doubt in my mind, though. I knew I had felt rejected by him, and once I accepted it, the curtain started to rise.

The Root

I could see my life play out, perceived rejection after perceived rejection. A long succession of painful memories passed by me like pieces in an assembly line. I understood that I had felt unlovable my entire life because of the deep hurt I felt when my father rejected me as a child. There were more reasons that explained why I felt unworthy of love, but I didn't dive into those until much later.

I flew home to Charleston and visited my mom, whom I had brought to live in the USA a year prior. I sat down with her and told her that even though I had no conscious recollection, I felt my father had rejected me and that he didn't want me. To my surprise, she started to cry and said, "How do you know?"

It turned out that my father's first words to my mother after she told him she was expecting me were: "Another problem to deal with."

My dad was not happy about my existence. I was right all those years when I felt I needed to earn my father's love. A love that should have been given to me freely and unconditionally but wasn't.

The Sanctity of the Grave

Acknowledging the harm caused by a living parent is difficult. Still, holding that parent accountable once they have passed away becomes more complex.

Susan Forward, Ph.D., is an American psychologist, psychotherapist, and author known for her work in the field of psychology, particularly in dysfunctional family dynamics and relationships. In her book *Toxic Parents: Overcoming Their Hurtful Legacy and Reclaiming Your Life*, she explains: "There's a powerful taboo against criticizing the dead, as if we were kicking them while they're down. As a result, death imparts a sort of sainthood to even the worst abuser. The deification of dead parents is almost automatic. Unfortunately, while the toxic parent is protected by the sanctity of the grave, the survivors are stuck with the emotional remains. Don't speak ill of the dead may be a treasured platitude, but it often inhibits the realistic resolution of conflicts with dead parents."

Death has a way of casting a halo over your memories of loved ones, including those who may have caused you pain and hardship.

I revered my father as a good and perfect parent throughout most of my life. His death placed him on top of an untouchable pedestal. He came down eventually, but not yet.

Opening a Can of Worms

In his book *Awaken the Giant Within*, Tony Robbins writes that a belief is a feeling of certainty about something. He likens a belief to a table. The legs of the table are the references you collect to validate your idea into a belief.

He points out that beliefs can be formed about almost anything if you gather sufficient evidence and reference experiences to support them. Additionally, he explains that you can change a belief by introducing doubt. When you question or challenge one of the supporting reference experiences, your belief begins to shift.

Shining light on the root of my lack of self-worth allowed me to remove a few reference legs from my table. The belief that I was unlovable started to shift.

I am sure you have heard the expression "Opening a can of worms." That phrase seems to have been born in bait shops, where the fishermen would buy a can full of live worms.

Live worms were much better than dead worms as bait. They were also fabulous at escaping. So, when trying to fix one problem, catching more fish, the fisherman would end up with a new problem, fugitive worms. Much like the worms in an open can, my thoughts and emotions were set loose in my mind during that seminar.

Identifying my limiting beliefs was not enough to explain my behaviors or transform my life. My life spiraled down two more years. Another man had to enter my life before I was desperate enough to go on a much deeper exploration of my mind.

Be a Curious Reader

While reading the last few chapters you likely thought about your own parents and your relationship with them. Think of it as dusting off and reading an old book. Each page holds stories, memories, and emotions that have shaped you over the years.

This exploration is not about judging your parents or yourself. It's about understanding the chapters that have influenced your life's narrative. Embrace this journey like a curious reader, turning the pages to reveal the plot twists and character development that have made you who you are today.

As you read about the challenges and growth I encounter later, you can decide if you are ready to embark on a journey of deeper exploration. Every individual's path is unique, and in these pages, you may find the inspiration and insights you need to chart your own course toward a more fulfilling and empowered life.

CHAPTER 17
Emotional Home

"The best journeys in life are those that answer questions you never thought to ask."

– Rich Ridgeway

Picture thick woods on a winter day. Snow is coming down heavily; it's windy and miserable. In the distance, you see a stone cabin; it looks cozy. Smoke is coming out from the chimney, the blinds are drawn, and the door is ajar.

You walk down the snowy path, and finally, you make it to the entrance. You push the door open, and the warmth caresses the frozen skin on your face. You step in and see a very plush and inviting leather couch. There are blankets all around.

On the side table, there is even a steamy cup of hot chocolate with fluffy marshmallows spilling over. You can't believe you found this place. You are three years old, and this is the closest thing to heaven on earth you have ever experienced. You close the door behind you. You jump on the couch and grab that hot chocolate, and you feel safe. You decide you prefer to be in there rather than outside. The outside world is scary and cold.

That is how I built my emotional home.

Your Emotional Home

You have an emotional home too. You designed it, you built it, it has walls and a roof.

At the seminar, Tony Robbins explained that the brain loves the feeling of certainty and familiarity. You learned to cope with life by developing familiar habits as a child.

An emotional home is the place you habitually went to when you faced distress. He said that an emotional home or refuge is not necessarily a good place to be in; it is simply a place that feels safer than the outside world.

You built your emotional home with the help of the emotions you felt more frequently when you were a child. Those constant emotions became very familiar. The more familiar they became, the more comfortable you felt around them and the more you accepted them as part of who you are.

As an adult, you consciously or unconsciously try to maintain those emotions to keep your sense of identity. Having better or more productive feelings is actually more daunting.

147

Journey back to your childhood and reflect on the emotions that shaped your emotional home—the refuge you habitually retreated to when faced with distress.

Can you recall the emotions that accompanied you most frequently during your early years? How did those constant emotions become familiar and comforting to you? Did you cling to those emotions as you grew, even if they didn't benefit you?

Think about the moments in your childhood when you sought solace in your emotional home. What events or circumstances triggered your need for that familiar space?

Now, consider how this emotional home influences your adult life. Do you find yourself unconsciously returning to those same emotions when faced with challenges or stressors today? How does it impact your relationships, career, and overall well-being?

Sad and Angry

While at the seminar, I identified which two emotions helped me build my emotional home. My walls were made out of sadness, and my roof was made out of anger.

I also realized that when challenges arose, I not only sought refuge in my cabin in the woods, I actually had tools that led me directly to that safe haven.

One tool I relied on was songs with lyrics that resonated deeply and evoked strong emotions within me. Almost daily, I would listen to songs that plunged me into sadness or anger.

Despite the discomfort, those emotions were familiar. Inside my cabin in the woods, I could be myself—a sad, lonely and angry woman. I didn't have to pretend to be cheerful or successful.

The Appalachian Trail

I love hiking; life is like a hike we embark on as soon as the sperm meets the egg. My hike has been like the Appalachian Trail. This trail is long, approximately 2,190 miles. It is stunning and it passes through many landscapes, including mountains, forests, valleys, streams, and rivers.

Completing the entire trail typically takes several months. It offers a range of difficulty levels, from relatively easy stretches to more challenging sections with steep ascents and rugged terrain. As a treat, hikers enjoy breathtaking views from many peaks.

Even though hiking it alone is not recommended. I chose to hike alone. Well, not entirely alone. I had two hiking companions that would never leave my side. The same two primary emotions that helped me build my emotional home: sadness and anger. Ever since my father died and even further back, during all those years I didn't remember, those two companions were always by my side.

Wonderfully Sexy

Even though my hiking companions were unkind and broke my heart repeatedly, I didn't want them to leave. We hiked together, and when things got really rough, we all took refuge in the cabin in the woods.

Happiness felt as foreign as a cold front in the middle of summer. Happiness didn't belong to me; sometimes, I saw it pass by on the hiking path, looking wonderfully sexy.

I only dared touch the fringes of her dress, and like Jesus Christ, she would turn around and look at me and ask, "Who touched me?" I would stay quiet; I wouldn't say, "It was me. I touched you; let's hike together." So, she would just keep on walking.

I reached a few peaks during my life's hike and enjoyed the breathtaking views of blessings. I took photos along the way, and those photos became memories. Yet, every time

I reached a summit, instead of looking at the majestic view, I would look towards the horizon and stare at the looming stormy clouds. Invariably, the gray clouds would come in and obscure the view. I was more comfortable in the fog.

Your Hike

What does your hike look like? What companions do you have on your life's journey? Are they supportive and kind, or do they contribute to your heartache and challenges? Consider the landscapes you encounter on your hike. Do you focus on potential negatives or uncertainties?

Remember, what you focus on shapes your reality. Your thoughts, beliefs, and where you put your attention influences what you experience and the results you bring into your life.

Recognizing the need for change and being honest with yourself about what must to be transformed are the first vital steps on your journey of personal growth. The fact that you are reading this book proves that you are searching for something; even if your brain doesn't know what it is, your soul knows!

A Flicker of Hope

I lived my life with a constant knot in my throat. I felt something was wrong with me, and I didn't belong in the world. I never let anyone get close. I often looked at my hand and wondered why I couldn't even name five people I loved. I knew something was amiss, yet I had never been to a psychiatrist or taken prescription drugs, so I brushed my feelings off.

Fueled by a flicker of hope after my initial Tony Robbins seminar, I stepped outside my comfort zone. Left the familiar behind and embraced new connections and a world of possibilities.

Yet, the road to recovery was far from linear. Sadness, that old companion, lurked in the shadows, ever ready to reclaim its grip on my weary soul.

CHAPTER 18
Hurricane Warning

"Waiting is painful. Forgetting is painful. But not knowing which to do is the worst kind of suffering."

– Paulo Coelho

Soul recognition is a feeling of "knowing" or "remembering" someone at a deeper level as if you have known them before.

Soulmates are people who act like a mirror for you. They have a special way of showing you the things that are holding you back in life.

They help you see parts of yourself that you may not have noticed. Seeing these parts is often challenging and uncomfortable. Choosing to grow from your interactions with soul mates is worth the effort. It helps you become the best version of yourself and live a more fulfilling life.

Paying Money to Make Friends

At the Tony Robbins's seminar, they pitched something called the Platinum Club. It appealed to me because I had no friends.

The club seemed like a great place to meet people. The members got to travel the world for a year, attending events covering various topics, including personal development, relationships, career, health, and finances. The membership also gave access to three exclusive events.

I wanted to learn new things, but most of all, I paid a lot of money to make friends. I didn't want to hike the Appalachian Trail with the two companions I had. I wanted to find new hiking partners.

Kismet

During my first Platinum Partnership event, my life changed. I went to the hotel bar for a drink and saw a man standing there. When I approached him, I experienced my first soul recognition.

His name was David, and I felt there was a strong bond between us that transcended time and space. Time stopped when I said hello, and he smiled. To me, it was as if the magnetic poles of the universe had come alive, and I was being pulled in his direction.

I had never experienced anything like it. I had been around handsome men, successful men, sweet men, interesting men, and a mix of all of the above. This was different; he emanated a kind of light I couldn't look away from.

David was like an oak tree planted by streams of water, and I was happy just being a bird sitting on one of its branches. He cast a beautifully safe shade over me.

I have had to fend for myself since I was a little girl. I always wanted my prince to show up on his white horse, sweep me off my feet, and look after me.

I waited on the castle's balcony for years with no sign of him. David was the closest thing to a prince I had ever met. And for a while, I thought he had come to save me.

The Friend Zone

We rode a bus up to the mountain the night we met. The ride lasted about 30 minutes. My mouth was a waterfall. I was telling him the story of my life. I don't think he realized how meaningful that was for me. After all, I was the woman who didn't open up to anyone. Not even to my closest family members.

There was an event nearly every month during that Platinum Year, so we attended events all over the world.

We became good friends. Our life circumstances did not allow for anything more. He was married and on the cusp of major life changes, and I was going through my divorce.

Rightly so, he planted me firmly in the friend zone. I didn't want to forget, so I grabbed an imaginary sticky note, wrote the word "friend" in big bold letters on it, and put it on his forehead.

Battered and Bruised

During one of the trips, I told him: "Once you re-organize your life, you should let me love you because I think I could." I had never felt that way.

Before I met David, love was as foreign to me as a tourist walking around Rome with his Hawaiian shirt, camera around his neck, and flip-flops with tall white socks.

However, when I met him, there was a glimmer of hope. I felt that, in his presence, I could eventually open up. I felt I could love him and that, finally, someone would love me in return.

One night, a few months after meeting him, I was watching synchronized swimmers performing beautiful aquatic ballet on TV when I had an epiphany. Underwater, synchronized swimming is a war zone; there are kicks, slaps, and collisions. On the surface, it looks calm, collected, and artistic.

I felt like one of those swimmers. I kept a harmonious and happy charade on the surface; underwater, I felt battered and bruised from the emotional war going on inside of me. I was being kicked by my own expectations and ideas. I had forgotten about the sticky note.

Your Inner Turmoil

Can you remember moments when you presented a harmonious and happy exterior while feeling emotionally battered and bruised? Here is what reflecting on those times can teach you:

1. **Self-awareness:** Remembering those moments helps you become more aware of your emotions and how you respond to them. It's like looking in a mirror to see what's really going on inside you.

2. **Patterns:** When you think about times when you've hidden your true feelings, you might notice patterns. You could discover that you tend to bottle up your emotions, put on a brave face, or avoid confronting your feelings.

3. **Coping mechanisms:** Reflecting on how you handled those tough moments can show you the strategies you used to cope. Did you distract yourself, talk to someone, or engage in a hobby? Recognizing these strategies can help you understand how you typically manage stress or sadness.

4. **Insights:** Analyzing these experiences can provide insights into why you reacted the way you did. Maybe you felt pressure to seem happy because you didn't want to burden others, or perhaps you were trying to keep up appearances.

5. **Growth:** Understanding how you coped in the past can guide you in making better choices in the future. You can learn from what worked and what didn't and develop healthier ways to manage your emotions.

6. **Empathy:** This reflection can also make you more empathetic towards others. When you realize how challenging it can be to hide your emotions, you might become more understanding of people who seem okay on the outside but are struggling inside.

Building a Tropical Hut

Even though I was bewildered by the situation with David, I worked hard in all the seminars I attended during my Platinum Year to build a new emotional home.

I am a tropical woman. I wanted my emotional refuge to be a hut on a Caribbean Island, surrounded by nothing more than white sand and palm trees. I didn't want blinds on my windows; the sunlight would come in instead.

I hung beautiful works of art painted by my mom on all the walls. I put in a chair, and I called it gratitude. I brought in a beautiful coffee table which I called hope.

I thought, "When things get hard, I am just going to go in there, sit on my chair of gratitude, put my sandy, barefoot feet on top of my table of hope, lean back and watch the sunset."

Unfortunately, when things got hard, I didn't do that.

Blood Dripping Down

When the Platinum Year ended, David went on to get a divorce and disappeared from my life. I quickly realized that my tropical hut was built on quicksand.

I again found myself walking down the familiar snowy path straight into my old cabin in the woods. I sat there for a long time, feeling lonely, angry, and sad.

During those years, living my life was like going down a slide covered in blades. I could feel the cuts, the warm blood dripping down my legs. I patched them up with bandages of fancy travels and distractions. Most of all, I disinfected the cuts with wine. I over-drank every day for two years straight.

My Glass Cage

I built a cage with empty wine bottles and didn't think I could escape it. I didn't understand what I was feeling. I was completely opposed to the idea of having fallen in love with David, so I just focused on his rejection as a reflection of my worth.

Even though I consciously understood that my feelings of unworthiness were based on my perceptions and interpretations rather than objective reality, I was hurting. Whatever I had uncovered during my seminars and what I had learned reading self-help books was not enough to make me happy. For a long time, I didn't do anything more to heal and grow; I just wallowed in my misery. The truth is that I had no clue what to do.

One night, I got drunk and decided to drive my golf cart down to the beach, and I took my French Bulldogs, Coco and Bombon. One of my pups rolled off the seat and onto the street. She could have died.

The following day, I sat on my bed and apologized to them. As I said, "I am sorry," they looked at me with their big eyes and quickly snored back to sleep.

I was faced with a choice: ignore that I was walking on a dangerous tightrope and about to fall, or do something radically different in my life. I was at a bottom, but I knew it was not rock bottom yet. Thankfully I chose to get off the tightrope before I hit rock bottom.

Pulling Out a New Book

The closest thing to a journal I had kept were my Instagram posts. However, the descriptions of my posts didn't match my reality. That morning, I must have been really desperate because I took a notebook out and finally wrote an honest note to myself:

"My heart is full and empty at the same time. I am scared; I have no one to talk to. I feel so alone. I have a life most people only dream of. I have experienced incredible adventures. I am grateful beyond words for my life's blessings.

Today feels like an ending and a beginning at the same time. I just moved into my amazing new house. I never thought I would live in such a gorgeous place. I fear that I will sit in it alone. I will, I know. I will scroll down on social media until it tells me I'm caught up and drink expensive wine until I am drunk.

I don't want that. My life is not perfect, and it scares me, but I will search for my future. I am pulling out a new book, one full of blank pages. I will find something to help me. I will find my purpose, something I love."

Writing things down is like making a wish to the universe. You jot down your thoughts, dreams, and wishes, and suddenly, they feel more real and achievable. There's this saying, "Writing it down makes it real."

When you write, you're not just scribbling words; you're creating a roadmap for your dreams. Your journal becomes a treasure map, and your words? They're like the 'open sesame' to making things happen. The words I wrote in my notebook that day turned my wishes into wonderful realities.

Picking Up the Phone

Just as a hurricane can cause significant environmental changes, David swept into my life, bringing intense emotions and new experiences that left an indelible mark. He nudged me to reshape my world entirely.

John Stix is an Identity Author, Speaker, and Transformation Specialist. He illustrates how we often ignore our calls to embark on self-exploratory adventures in his book *Discover Your WHO: Ignite the Answers Within and Reinvent Your Life*: "Imagine yourself walking down the path of your life. Along the path are phone booths, lined up, one after the other. And as you walk past them, the phone inside the first booth is ringing. You have the choice to walk past or stop and pick up the phone. If you walk past, another phone booth with a ringing phone soon comes into view. Sometimes the phones are harder to hear. Sometimes you just ignore them. But always, there's another one ringing. These phones are connected to your authentic self, who has a message for you about your true purpose, who wants to tell you that the things you're chasing in life aren't connected to who you really are."

I had ignored the signs and patterns that kept showing up on my life's hike. My self-harming behaviors, fears, inability to feel beautiful emotions, and my persistent feelings of disconnection. But I finally walked by a phone that rang so loud, I couldn't ignore the call anymore.

The universe sent David to shake me, so I could get the message to dig deeper into my soul. I had the pieces of the puzzle laid in front of me, and the time to put them back together was closer than I thought.

You Call

What calls have you heard in your life urging you to take a leap of faith and embark on a transformational journey? How has your journey been affected by the ones you embraced versus the ones you ignored?

Consider the calls that lie ahead. How might answering future calls shape the person you are becoming or challenge the perception of who you think you are?

Take a moment to pause, listen, and pick up that one phone call that can lead you to the answers within. It might just unravel what is blocking you from living a life of love and fulfillment.

Hidden Memories

PART 2
The Catalyst of Transformation

"A good life is one hero journey after another. Over and over again, you are called to the realm of adventure, you are called to new horizons. Each time, there is the same problem: do I dare? And then if you do dare, the dangers are there, and the help also, in the fulfillment or the fiasco."

– Joseph Campbell

Life is made up of a succession of adventures. The adventures often look like the hero journey described by Joseph Campbell on the quote above. The next parts of this book are about my hero journey.

Here is a quick preview:

Once upon a time, there was a brave young girl. She was an ordinary kid, but destiny called her to embark on a great adventure. Her journey began when she received a special call. She needed to save herself from darkness and to ultimately find a magical treasure.

She faced many challenges, scary monsters, and walked treacherous paths. But she also made new friends, learned invaluable lessons, and discovered her inner strength.

With courage, determination, kindness, and grace, she overcame obstacles, grew wiser, and found the power to bring hope and happiness to her inner and outer world. And in the end, she returned home with treasures and elixirs and shared them with the world.

Your Reflections

Be prepared to embark on an adventure that might resonate with the essence of your own life. Like the brave young girl in the story above, you too have embarked on countless journeys, each with its own challenges, triumphs, and transformative moments. I invite you to:

- Reflect upon the treacherous paths you've traversed, the monsters you've faced, and the friendships that have illuminated your path.
- Consider the invaluable lessons you've learned along the way and the strength that resides within you.
- Allow yourself to draw parallels between your own heroic journey and the tale unfolding before you.
- Discover the treasures you've gained, the elixirs of wisdom that have nourished your soul, and the power you possess to bring hope and happiness to your inner and outer world.
- Challenge your perceptions and beliefs, embracing introspection and growth with every turn of the page.
- Find inspiration to overcome your own obstacles and create your narrative of triumph, love, and fulfillment.

May my journey serve as a reminder that within you lies the potential for extraordinary growth, resilience, and the ability to create a life of profound meaning.

CHAPTER 19
Drilling Expedition

"When we have the courage to walk into our story and own it, we get to write the ending."

– Brené Brown

Sometimes life shows you a different path. One that you didn't know you were ever supposed to walk on. You can resist it, discount it, and try to remain the same. Or you can embrace it and walk on it one step at a time. Full of curiosity and fear, each step takes you closer and closer to the person you were always supposed to be. Each stride reminds you of who you truly are.

I was scared of anything that could be remotely extraordinary. I was raised to believe that all that was unexplainable was, by default, black magic or demonic. That belief was engraved on me as superficially and permanently as the ink of a tattoo.

After the incident with my dogs, I put aside my fears and apprehensions and booked a plane ticket to Costa Rica. I was told by close friends about a retreat there where people healed their hearts. I was heartbroken, so I figured that would be a good place to start.

I didn't realize it then, but I went there to heal more than my heart. I was going to heal my body and my mind.

My Feet Ready to Run

The place is called Rythmia; it's about one hour away from Liberia. As soon as I arrived, I was submerged in a curriculum of classes and lessons.

It was like I had just stepped into a university of healing. They gave us knowledge, skills, and tools to navigate the journey we were about to embark on.

I checked into Rythmia with a head full of doubts and my feet ready to run. I felt a sense of peace when I walked the gravel path down to my room during my first afternoon there.

The alarms going off in my mind for the last few years quieted down. The wind was caressing the branches of the trees, and the leaves were dancing. I relaxed.

All of a sudden, I saw the path behind me as clear as day. I saw how the steps I had taken the last years, all those seminars I attended, and the books I read were preparing me for this time.

Even though I didn't know it then, my life's difficulties had been pop-quizzes meant to sharpen me to face the difficulties that were about to come.

Perhaps your past challenges have also been preparing you for a future of further growth and discovery.

Mrs. Moon

Early the following morning, I walked the literal path from my bedroom to a classroom to attend a talk called *About Your Miracle*. "I don't believe in miracles," I thought as I entered the room.

A witty man addressed the class. "Oh man, another charming man with salt-n-pepper hair. Have I really come this long way just to get sidetracked again?" I thought in disbelief.

He delineated his life story in a comical yet vulnerable way as if we were all sitting on a cool night around a fire, hearing a storyteller tell his fantastic tale.

Listening to his story unfold did exactly what stories are meant to do. It inspired me to open my mind more fully. It forced me to compare our paths and allowed me to find similarities and differences. And most of all, the story of the transformation of his spirit and heart gave me hope. I had not felt hope in a long time.

He described talking to the moon. The moon showed him who he had become and, more dramatically, why he had become that man.

I wanted to hear what the moon would tell me, but I was afraid of sinning against God, I hoped that what I was about to do was not a sin.

Later that night, we would have the first of four plant medicine ceremonies. That sounded too ominous and religious, so I settled on the phrase medical treatment.

Plant medicine refers to using various plants, their parts, or extracts for medicinal purposes.

Stepping into the Unknown

I entered the room at 5:30 p.m. The whole place was bathed with a sweet-smelling smoke. There were many neatly organized mattresses on the floor, and I picked one of them. I sat on my crisp white sheet, rearranged my pillow, and placed it against the wood beam behind me.

I located the bucket at my feet and the roll of toilet paper they told us we would have. I unfolded the soft blanket that would become my best friend and enemy during the night.

More people filed in one by one. I saw my own face in their faces, our expectant eyes and tight mouths. Every step they took mirrored my own, filled with hope and anxiety.

Stirred Like a Martini

After our previous orientation, we were left feeling stirred, much like a martini, with abundant information. However, the reassurances we received had been perfectly mixed in, resulting in a velvety smooth texture.

The waiting seemed to last for hours. The energy in the room kept ramping up. I became more and more anxious. Desperation had brought me there. I was yearning for something, anything that could help me.

The thought of not feeling anything scared me, I didn't want to feel dead inside anymore. I was already disconnected from my body, God, my feelings, from those whom I should love, and from life. "It can't get any worse," I thought.

Finally, the man serving the medicine explained that they would serve several rounds of medicine and that the treatment would go until 2 a.m. Lastly, he gave us some final recommendations and a safety briefing.

People dressed in funny outfits started to sing beautiful songs and to blow smoke onto large jars containing a dark liquid.

I had walked the streets of Varanasi, seen people shot next to me in Venezuela, and carried a rock star in my arms like a baby (yes, that did happen, I swear). Yet, sitting on my mattress that night was as far out of my comfort zone as I had ever been.

In Front of a Medicine Man

I have always had a need to be first, first in everything. My goal in school was not just to get a perfect score but also to hand in my test and leave the room first. When I enter concerts, I don't just want to be in the front; I want to take the best spot. In the self-development seminars, I am the first one rushing in to take the best chair.

This night was no different. As soon as they called for the first cup, I sprinted from my mattress and was first in line. I held a little empty shot glass in my hand.

I handed the man my empty cup, and a few seconds later, he handed it back to me. It was filled to the rim with a thick-looking brown concoction. He placed it between my fingers, looked into my eyes, and said, "Have a good journey, sister." I guess he knew I was on a journey, even when I didn't.

Who Am I?

In the class that morning, they explained the importance of having a clear intention for each cup we drank. If I hadn't attended that morning's lesson, my intention would have been, "Help me find a purpose," or "Help me understand why I chase unavailable men."

But in class, they guided us towards a much more useful and thought-provoking first intention; it was simple yet compelling: "Show me who I have become." Most of us go through life having no clue of who we are. When I asked the question, "Who am I?" I answered in my head:

"I am a business woman."

"I am Hispanic."

"I am sad and lonely."

"I am a daughter and a sister."

"I am determined."

"I am too impatient," and so on.

But those sentences didn't really define who I was at my core. The truth is that I didn't know who I was.

Who Are You?

Not knowing who you truly are has profound negative effects on your life. When you can't identify your core essence, you may define yourself by external roles, appearances, or fleeting emotions. These surface-level labels can lead you to build a fragile sense of identity and leave you vulnerable to the whims of circumstances and other people's opinions.

If you find yourself unsure of who you are, you are not alone. Your journey of self-discovery might be complex, but it's one of the most rewarding paths you'll ever tread. Picture each step as an opportunity to peel away layers, gaining insights into what truly resonates with you. What brings you joy? What ignites your passions? What values do you hold dear?

Remember, self-discovery is not just about understanding who you are today; it's about realizing the potential of who you can become. With newfound clarity, you can make choices that resonate deeply with your core, leading to a more genuine and purposeful life.

Digging from Chile to China

"Show me who I have become." That little, seemingly simple intention was like a drill that made a hole in the surface of my heart, right down to my heart's crust and beyond.

I started my drilling expedition that night. Drilling through my heart was like drilling from Chile to China. It was challenging. Drilling deep into my heart was akin to drilling though the earth's crust.

At 13,000 ft. deep, it got really hot. At around 130,000 feet, the temperature was an excruciating 1832 Fahrenheit. It was so hot that the rocks became soft. It felt like I was journeying through a furnace of challenges.

But amidst this hardship, something magical happened. I reached a layer where the intense heat and pressure had worked their magic, giving birth to countless breathtaking diamonds. Their beauty mesmerized me, reminding me of the miracles hidden within life's toughest moments.

Yet, the true test still lay ahead. The solid iron core stood defiant, almost impossible to break through. And even when I triumphed over that barrier, I realized I was only at the halfway mark.

Gravity played tricks on my senses, leaving me disoriented and weary; at times, I felt I was going backward. There were moments when doubt threatened to consume me, and the weight of uncertainty felt insurmountable.

With every ounce of strength and hope, I pressed on. My journey led me to unearth more precious jewels, each a reminder that even amidst life's most trying layers, profound beauty lies waiting to be discovered.

That first treatment and first cup started the journey that tested the very core of my being. The expedition lasted many months, and it involved many different treatments and experiences. But the drill eventually breached the surface on the other side of my heart. I made it to my own personal "China", forever transformed by the resilience it took to arrive.

Unearthing Your Truths

Take a moment to reflect on your journey of self-discovery—past, present, and future. Have you encountered moments where life's challenges felt like an intense furnace, pushing you to your limits? What precious diamonds have you unearthed amidst the toughest layers of your life? Or, perhaps, if your deepest expedition lies ahead, ask yourself: What truths are waiting to be unearthed? What glimmers of hope and resilience will guide you?

CHAPTER 20
Intelligent Medicine

"Courage is a love affair with the unknown."

– Osho

Knowing what will happen once you drink the liquid is virtually impossible. And after you do, it's impossible to shake the feeling that you have been touched by an intelligent representative of the natural world.

Ayahuasca

The substance I drank is the plant medicine called ayahuasca. Ayahuasca is a brew made up of two plants that have been used for centuries by indigenous cultures.

One is a vine, and the other is a plant with a powerful psychedelic compound called DMT.

The term "psychedelics" comes from ancient Greek. "Psyche" means "mind," and "deloun" means "to make visible" or "to reveal." So, a psychedelic substance is like a tool that opens the door to exploring your thoughts and feelings from a new angle, giving you fresh insights and understandings.

The experience with ayahuasca is often described as an exploration of one's consciousness. It can bring about a range of effects, vivid visuals, profound sensory experiences, and a heightened sense of self-awareness. It is, generally, extremely intense.

A Bucket Full of Vomit

Ayahuasca is highly purgative. During treatments, the bucket at your feet becomes your most precious possession; you find yourself taking your bucket wherever you go. It is almost comical to watch grown adults stumbling around in the dark, holding on to a bucket full of vomit as if it holds the secrets of their universe, and maybe it does.

Science gives a rational explanation for this phenomenon. The purging occurs due to the ayahuasca's influence on the area of the brain stem that controls the urge to throw up. The medicine acts on serotonin receptors in that area of the brain and in the gut, causing vomiting, nausea, and diarrhea.

During the treatments, vomiting seems to come as strongly and suddenly as a tornado. Being in the ceremony is akin to being in the middle of a storm. You might feel drops falling on your face and observe the black clouds on the horizon. Yet, nothing prepares you for the funnel-shaped cloud that emerges, reaching the ground with 300 mph winds.

Not a Normal Puke

This type of vomiting feels nothing like a normal puke. The purge feels as if the tornado suddenly and forcefully makes its way into your stomach and spins there, destroying perceptions, emotions, and past experiences.

Each cup has an objective; this tornado liquefies all that is necessary to clear the path for insights and healing to come. With irreverent force from the root of your being, this tornado turns into a volcano, erupting out of your mouth with sounds that can be heard as far as the stars.

Science can't explain why you often know the specific thoughts or emotions you are purging when you go through that violent process. You can almost see them take shape in the bucket; sometimes, they do.

Fear of Purging

It's quite common for people to have concerns about the possibility of vomiting during an ayahuasca treatment. However, it's important to recognize that while this aspect can be challenging, there are significant benefits to the overall experience. It's also worth noting that other aspects of the ayahuasca journey hold greater importance.

Purging is considered a part of the healing process in ayahuasca ceremonies. It releases physical and emotional toxins from the body, symbolizing a cleansing of both the physical and spiritual self. Although it can be uncomfortable, many people report feeling a sense of relief and lightness afterward.

Embracing the entire experience with an open mind and a willingness to confront discomfort can lead to significant positive changes and a deeper understanding of yourself and the world.

Nothing Short of Magic

I once heard that there are two types of medicines, intelligent and non-intelligent. You take non-intelligent medicine with a specific, predetermined outcome in mind; it is usually synthetic. If you get a headache, you take an aspirin, knowing that it will take the ache away. If indigestion strikes, taking an antacid often soothes your discomfort.

Intelligent medicine, like ayahuasca, is nothing short of magic. You take it, and even if you have an outcome in mind, the medicine does what you need instead of what you want.

In my treatments, I have met many agnostics. When they are done, they might not believe in God still, but they know there is more out there than they thought.

Broken Beyond Repair

Smoke and music filled the air in the room as I held the small cup in my hands. I didn't allow myself to think about what I was about to do. I just whispered into the cup, "Show me who I have become." And in one swift gulp, I swallowed the liquid.

The flavor of the foul-tasting liquid lingered in my mouth. I fought back my normally dormant gag reflex, sat on my mattress, and watched the long line of people in front of me. Each person grabbed their first cup and walked back to their mattress.

The lights went down. It felt as if the seconds were minutes and the minutes were hours. I waited. About 20 minutes in, loud noises disrupted the air; harrowing cries and loud purging sounds put me on edge.

I recalled The Dickens Process and the sounds I had heard in that arena three years before. Although we were only about 70 people in Costa Rica, the sounds were worse.

I thought if hell existed, I had stepped through its gates, and I was taking in the sobs of all civilization from the beginning of time.

183

Hours passed, and many around me were shaking, crying, sweating, vomiting, and rushing to the bathroom, but I felt... nothing.

"I told you it was a waste of time to come here," said the negative voice in my head.

"You must be broken beyond repair if not even this thing can make you feel something," it added.

When I heard the call for the second cup, I put all those doubts aside. And as if propelled by a spring, I landed right in front of the medicine man.

Once again, I lifted the cup to my lips and said, this time with more conviction, "Show me who I have become." And then my life started to change.

Your Fears

It's completely understandable to have reservations and fear about delving deep into your own stories and about embarking on a self-discovery journey.

You might wonder: What if I uncover painful memories or emotions I can't handle? What if I open up old wounds I've worked hard to bury? What if I don't like what I find? These are valid concerns, and it's essential to honor and acknowledge them.

However, refusing to treat a wound doesn't make it disappear; it continues to hurt, fester, and may even lead to systemic problems that impact all aspects of your life. Like a physical wound, emotional and psychological wounds demand your attention and care.

The fear is often rooted in a lack of information and understanding about the process or the potential effects of healing treatments, including psychedelics.

It's natural to feel hesitant about exploring unknown territory, especially if you aren't fully aware of what to expect or how the process works. As you read further in this book, you will find valuable tips and insights that shed light on the healing process, the effects of psychedelics, and what to anticipate during treatments.

In addition to the positive aspects, this book also includes valuable warnings and recommendations to ensure you are well informed about potential risks and challenges.

Remember that your path of self-discovery is entirely your own. Whether you choose to take small steps or leap into the depths with the help of healing substances, always be gentle with yourself and honor your unique process.

CHAPTER 21
Guilt and Shame

"Everything is energy and that's all there is to it."
– Albert Einstein

Growing up, my mother described the chilling sound the chains made when my brother's casket was lowered into the ground. I didn't understand how that sound stabs the heart until I heard it on the day of my father's funeral.

I was transported to that day with my second cup of medicine.

When the treatment started, it looked like the waters of energy were all around me. Yet, I felt nothing. It was as if I was a hermetically sealed submarine. Opening up to this unknown field was as difficult as opening a porthole underwater.

I thought that the whole concept of energy was woo-woo nonsense. I didn't believe in miracles.

After taking my second cup, I walked out and stood by a bonfire. One of the helpers came out and stood behind me. She started to lightly touch my back. She said, "Stop fighting, let the energy flow. Connect."

As I heard that word and looked at the flames, their color and intensity changed. A current of energy traveled from the crown of my head down my spine all the way to my sacrum. I felt the vertebrae on my spine move one by one very fast.

I took a deep breath. I didn't actually breathe in, something in me did. It felt as if my soul had been gasping for air all along, and at that moment, I took the plastic bag off its head, and it breathed for the first time ever.

I Came to Suffer

I went back inside, laid down on my mattress, and heard the most beautiful melodies. I could see music, really see it, in all its splendor. All the colors of the universe merged into a dance in front of my eyes. I felt very small in front of all its beauty.

Then, out of nowhere, anger welled up inside of me. I felt a rush of intense emotions and tension. I screamed, "NO, I DIDN'T COME HERE TO FEEL GOOD; I CAME HERE TO SUFFER."

Deep within, I clung to the belief that healing could only be experienced on the other side of suffering, my suffering.

All the beauty and the colors stopped instantly. I felt cold, as if I was lying on an iceberg in the middle of the arctic circle. I shivered from my core.

The Edge of the Abyss

In need of warmth and searching for comfort, I reached for the fluffy blanket. As I did, I remembered what they had said in the orientation that morning: "Don't get too comfortable. The more uncomfortable you get, the closer you are to the edge of the abyss of discovery."

So, I pulled the blanket off me and said loudly, "I WANT TO BE COLD." I laid there with every muscle of my body fully engaged. Shaking like I had never shaken before.

I braced for impact and waited for the edge of my abyss to appear. A few minutes later, the cold turned into heat, and I curled up like a child and wept. Outcries came out of my lungs, and I struggled to get the air back into them. Sobs turned into wails of pain.

Guilt and Shame

I was transported to the day we buried my father. I could feel the grass beneath my shoes. I stood in the cemetery surrounded by the hundreds of people who attended his burial. His casket was suspended by chains right in front of me.

I replayed the events of his burial in my head. I remembered that as they lowered the casket, I launched myself onto the top of it. I felt hands on my shoulders holding me back. On that day, while crying bitterly, I grabbed a handful of dirt and threw it on the casket.

I felt so much pressure, I was underwater in my closed submarine. Being transported to my father's burial was akin to a missile hitting its side. When the water rushed in, I threw myself on top of my bucket, and I purged. Guilt and shame left my body at full speed.

I could almost see stars inside that bucket. Once finished, I sat back and felt an immense relief. Something had changed; an old belief had changed. Healing was not reserved for other people, after all. "I can heal too," I whispered. I closed my eyes and fell asleep.

A Sight to Behold

An hour or so later, the lights came on. People were slowly coming back from wherever the medicine had taken them.

The end of a ceremony is a sight to behold. The once neat room is in total disarray. The once pristine sheets and buckets are not clean anymore.

People were lying in various positions, their bodies finding comfort in unconventional ways.

Some people appeared utterly confused; their faces reflected a sense of bewilderment. Others looked shocked; their expressions revealed the impact of what they had experienced.

After the treatments, there is always a sharing session where individuals can ask questions or discuss their experiences. These sessions can be incredibly healing, providing a space for listening to others and realizing that our lives and experiences often bear similarities.

Through hearing the stories of others, you can find solace, connection, and a sense of understanding that contributes to your own healing process. I didn't share that night, and I didn't listen to the shares either. I was too immersed in my thoughts. I felt exhausted and confused.

Mystery and Wonder

As I walked back to my room, I felt the wet grass and earth under my feet. I was confused as to what had happened. It made sense for the medicine to take me back to something related to my father. His death had shattered me, but why had the medicine taken me back to that day?

I asked myself: "Why did I feel those emotions? Did it show me who I had become? Who was I? A frightened girl full of guilt and shame?" I was able to make sense of it about a year later.

That night, all I understood was that I had opened a door, and ayahuasca was my ally.

That moment by the fire, when I felt energy run down my spine, was a tiny occurrence that profoundly altered my life's path. It gave me faith in the unknown. In that instant, I became a believer in the extraordinary.

When you let go of fear, amazing things can happen. You can find yourself in a place of mystery and wonder. I was in such a place when the night ended.

Hidden Memories

CHAPTER 22
A Roller Coaster

"The scars you can't see are the hardest to heal."
– Astrid Alauda

When I was a kid, I was fascinated by roller coasters. They made me feel brave and grown up.

Why do so many people like roller coasters after all? They make you feel alive. They produce a mix of joy, excitement, delight, terror, and happiness.

The best roller coasters have a very slow ascent, which allows the emotions to build. And they always have a short pause at the very top.

Fear and excitement can cause similar physiological responses in the body. So much so that you cannot differentiate between the two emotions when you are at the highest point waiting for the drop. It is as if you feel them both at the same time.

On the second night in Rythmia, as I stepped into the treatment room, I felt like a wide-eyed kid perched atop a towering roller coaster, anticipating that exhilarating drop.

An Emotional Kaleidoscope

The room seemed to pulsate with energy, and the air was charged with anticipation. My heart pounded as I braced myself for whatever lay ahead. The unknown carried the promise of transformation and the uncertainty of challenges.

Unlike the previous night, I felt the medicine's effect after just one cup. The world around me took on a surreal hue, and my senses seemed to sharpen, making every sound, sight, and touch more vibrant and profound.

I felt connected to the present moment, my body, and the energy that permeated the room. I transcended the boundaries of my everyday self, opening the door to a heightened state of awareness and understanding.

The medicine's influence on my emotions was profound. Waves of joy and trepidation bathed me, sometimes intertwining and other times clashing fiercely against each other. It was an emotional kaleidoscope, and I surrendered to its power, embracing the turmoil that came with it.

Mic Drop

As the medicine took hold, I thought about the painful feelings I had been struggling with for the last two years, my fears of rejection, and my lack of self-worth.

I asked: "Why do I attract these men who don't appreciate me? Why do I chase them and abandon myself along the way?"

A voice inside my head answered, "Because they are sad, unhappily married, successful, lonely, and have kids at home."

Confused, I asked, "Why is that important?"

"You want to fix them," the voice said.

"Why?" I asked.

"Because you couldn't fix your dad," the voice answered.

If I had been holding a microphone, that would have been the perfect time for a mic drop. It was a major aha moment.

Have you ever watched an optical illusion called the Rubin's vase? It is also known as the face or vase illusion. The central part of the image appears to depict a vase or urn. However, if you shift your focus and attention, you see two faces in profile looking at each other. Once you see one interpretation, it becomes difficult to switch to the other.

Some people see the two faces plainly and quickly. But for years, I was only able to see the vase. That night, the answers to those questions allowed me to see the two faces for the first time. I was able to understand the effects of my father's presence in my life from a different perspective. Still, nothing could have prepared me for what happened the next night.

The Failed Savior

In many cases, children who subconsciously or consciously believe they failed in saving their parents seek out individuals to rescue in their adult romantic relationships.

Abused or neglected children learn to settle for crumbs of affection. They confuse the thrill of uncertainty and effort with real love, which just messes up their idea of what love should be like.

As a child, I thought I had to earn my father's love. My adult mind believed my efforts would surely earn me the love of the men I wanted, especially if that love was hard to get. I was addicted to unavailable men.

Are You Settling?

As you reflect on these patterns and experiences, consider how your own childhood dynamics may have shaped your understanding of love and relationships. Have you noticed any recurring themes in your romantic choices? Are there patterns that echo the dynamics you experienced with your caregivers?

Take a moment to ponder whether settling for less than you deserve in relationships might be rooted in past feelings of inadequacy or a desire to earn love. How might this awareness transform your approach to love and intimacy?

Remember, recognizing these patterns is not about blame but about gaining insight and breaking free from harmful cycles.

My Electric Body

After taking the medicine, I lay on the mattress, and energy started to flow through my body; it felt like electricity. It traveled from my feet to my head, from my chest to my fingertips.

In his masterpiece, *The Untethered Soul*, author and spiritual teacher Michael Singer writes:

"The heart controls the energy flow by opening and closing. This means that a heart, like a valve, can either allow the flow of energy to pass through or it can restrict the flow of energy from passing through."

He explains that if we resist thoughts or emotions because they are disturbing, they get stuck and create an energy blockage deep in our hearts.

In the yogic tradition, that unfinished energy pattern is called a samskara. Samskara is an emotional or mental imprint left on the mind due to past experiences or actions. These impressions create deep-rooted patterns that influence your thoughts, emotions, and behaviors.

When I understood the root of one of the behaviors that had plunged me into despair so many times, a few of the samskaras that had been blocking my heart dissolved. The energy of my own heart bathed my body for hours that night. It was magnificent.

Discomfort in My Soul

Towards the end of the night, a sweet medicine woman came and sat by my side. I was shaking a lot. She put her hand on my head and caressed me. I relaxed and turned my head so my right ear rested on the pillow; she stroked my hair and said, "Good girl."

Something primal woke up in me when I heard those words. I didn't know why; I just felt a deep discomfort in my soul. My subconscious dropped another clue! Yet, I was still clueless.

The path to a more liberated and authentic self is not instantaneous; it unfolds step by step. My energy channels were opened in preparation for what was to come: the most difficult night of my life.

Hidden Memories

CHAPTER 23
Into the Depths

*"In the midst of winter, I found there was,
within me, an invincible summer."*

– Albert Camus

Twenty years, seven months, and ten days had passed
since my father's death.

As the sun dipped below the horizon on my third night
at Rythmia, I again found myself at the entrance to the
medicine room. The clock read 5:30 p.m., and I was ready for
my treatment. I didn't know what to ask or what I wanted my
intention to be. I still didn't know who I had become, so I held
that intention as I drank my first three cups.

A Blockage

As time went on, my initial excitement transformed into
frustration. Despite drinking three cups, I couldn't sense any
noticeable effects.

Doubts began to creep in, so I approached the woman
serving the medicine. "I've had three cups," I said, "but I
don't feel anything. Could I get a fourth?"

The woman met my gaze with empathy, her eyes
reflected a profound understanding of the complexities of the
inner journeys.

She said, "I sense you have a blockage; how is your
work?"

I said, "My work is fine."

She then asked, "What is your problem area in life?"

Without missing a beat, I said, "Men."

She then asked, "How is your relationship with your father?"

I said, "Good, I mean, he died...he was my best friend."

She said, "Why don't you go outside and release the memory of your father?"

The idea of releasing my father's memory, the very essence that connected me to him, stirred up a whirlwind of emotions inside me. I felt agitated, and tears welled in my eyes, threatening to spill over.

"I don't want to," I replied, my voice quivering with vulnerability. "If I do, does it mean he is gone?"

She lovingly explained, "No, it just means that you release him so he can be free, and you can be free. Once you are done, come back, and I will give you another cup." She then turned around to help the next person.

My Subconscious Spoke

Coming across ideas or concepts you haven't thought about before is common during psychedelic treatments. Sometimes, your subconscious mind can hold information or insights that have not fully surfaced to your conscious awareness. These hidden thoughts or knowledge may emerge at any time, during or after treatments, and carry powerful insights.

I walked outside holding my bucket; I flipped it and sat on it. The moon was full that night, much like the moon I looked at on the day of my father's wake.

199

Tears started to flow. I said, "Dad, you would be proud of me. I have done well; I have made a lot of money. I have a beautiful house, and I have traveled the world."

I looked at that full moon and uttered words that came from my subconscious mind. I said, "Dad, I have to let you go now. I am sending you to the moon because I want to love a man, and there is only space in my heart for you."

As I said those words, my whole body relaxed, and I wept. I wept because the words rang true.

Unknowingly, letting go of some part of him opened a door within me, a door that led to a space of truth.

The Hardest Cup

I walked back inside and got my last cup of the night. As I held it in my hands, words that could only have come from my subconscious mind left my lips again. I said, "This is the hardest cup I will ever drink."

I changed my intention, and I asked the medicine:

"Please help me remember the beautiful memories of my childhood; let me remember my dad. I miss him."

I lay on my mattress, and after some time, my hands were in front of my face. My fingers moved very fast, as though I was sorting through a Rolodex of memories.

Every so often, I pulled a memory out and looked at the card. They were all empty.

After what felt like hours, I grew tired and felt frustrated. My left hand lovingly held my right hand. I stared at my intertwined fingers in the dim light of the room, and a profound sense of recognition washed over me. It was as if I had discovered a hidden truth, a revelation waiting to be unveiled.

One hand belonged to my father, and the other was my own. As I ventured into the depths of my mind, a sudden and vivid image flashed in my mind's eye. The universe revealed a piece of my inner puzzle at that precise moment.

You Got it Wrong

The last two nights taught me that once a thought or image comes into your mind, it indicates where the medicine is taking you. So, when that unexpected image emerged, I sat up faster than I had ever sat up before, and I screamed: "NO, YOU FUCKING GOT IT WRONG."

I spoke to the medicine: "You got it wrong, fucking try again." And I laid back down. The same image came again a few seconds later. My voice was a mix of panic and pain, anger and shock. I just kept on saying: "NO, NOO, NOOO, NOOOO."

In those heart-wrenching moments, my soul knew everything, and every cell in my body carried the weight of remembrance. It was an agonizing experience, the most horrible instant of my life. My brain struggled to catch up.

The image was a penis. It was my father's penis.

Go or Be Dragged

In the classes, they mentioned that we only have two options when the medicine is taking us somewhere deep within our psyche. We either go, or we will be dragged.

I did not go.

For hours that night, I waged the most brutal and devastating war. I screamed, cried, and punched my mattress. It felt like I was in the middle of a battlefield, unprotected, taking fire from all sides, still standing.

I was reminded to breathe multiple times by the beautiful helpers. "I can't," I would tell them as I gasped for air. "I can't breathe."

But I could, and I did.

I became the most exhausted I have ever been. Every muscle of my body ached. I am blessed with a very athletic build; my muscles turned into Jell-O that night. I couldn't even lift my arm by the time the battle ended.

The Collapse of Everything

Still on my mattress, I sat back up. My entire body was a white flag of surrender.

A beautiful landscape of buildings and skyscrapers appeared before my eyes. Larger than New York's or Dubai's. It all fully collapsed inward in slow motion. I knew the landscape represented my life.

In that moment, I lost my identity. I realized that everything I had ever achieved was worthless. My life felt meaningless. I questioned all my beliefs. I was in the middle of a whirlpool. And for a hot minute, I wanted to drown.

What I did next remains, and likely will always be, one of the most important moments of the decision of my life. I accepted, whatever was to come, and stopped resisting. At that moment, my life re-started.

Your Grieving Process

Acceptance is one of the crucial stages of grief. The concept of the grieving process was first introduced by Elisabeth Kübler-Ross in her book *On Death and Dying*, where she identified five stages of grief: denial, anger, bargaining, depression, and acceptance.

In this model, acceptance is the final stage, where individuals come to terms with the reality of their loss or the complex emotions and experiences they are facing.

Acceptance doesn't necessarily mean that you are "okay" with what happened, but rather, you have come to understand and acknowledge it in a way that allows you to move forward in your life.

You can go through the five stages of grief during an Ayahuasca treatment. Or it might take you a while to arrive at the last stage and accept what came up during treatment.

The grieving process is not linear, and it's unique to you; you might move back and forth between different stages, and that's perfectly fine.

CHAPTER 24

My Warrior Soul

*"Nature loves courage. You make the commitment
and nature will respond to that commitment
by removing impossible obstacles."*

– Terence McKenna

My mind carried breadcrumbs of clues throughout my life, leading me to a truth hiding in plain sight. The image of that penis in a shower was not unfamiliar; it had appeared in my thoughts on numerous occasions well into my adult life.

I just always set it aside without giving it a second thought. I rationalized it, saying: "I probably saw him taking a shower one day." I had never read or been exposed to any resources that could explain why the image was there. I never asked.

Show Me; I Want to Know

I was wearing a T-shirt with short sleeves that night in Costa Rica. After I accepted and surrendered, I rolled up my invisible sleeves as if getting ready for a fistfight. But I was no longer fighting the medicine or myself. I was ready to fight for knowledge. I hit the mattress once with the palms of my hands and said with absolute determination, "Show me; I want to know."

The room was packed and very loud; everyone was going through their own processes. But when those words left my lips, it all became totally silent. And the space around me turned white. I was in the center of a quiet, white room.

I heard a sound come from behind me. Slowly, my "mental screen" flickered to life, and the process of remembering started.

I was shown pivotal moments of my childhood in a semi-linear timeline. The images were not visually clear. I could feel everything that was happening on the screen, but I wasn't being retraumatized by it.

My mouth dropped open as far as it could go, and my jaw locked up in that position. My eyes opened wide in shock as my head turned clockwise very slowly.

Each memory lingered on the screen until it was fully integrated by my conscious brain. Then, my mouth and eyes would close, and the room would become bright and loud again.

This process repeated itself with each memory and lasted for a long time.

Marilyn Monroe

After the initial shock passed and the treatment ended, I asked for my mattress to be brought out. I lay awake under the stars and the full moon until the morning. I was still in a hallucinatory state, so I saw Marilyn Monroe on the face of the moon; she kept me company that night.

I was plagued with questions. How is it possible that I didn't remember any of this? Why didn't I say anything when it started? Why did I not say anything after he died?

In Limbo

I couldn't bring myself to return home that week. The world I had known had shifted beneath my feet.

The familiar routines and environments of my life seemed foreign and distant. I questioned the reality I had constructed for myself until that point in my life. I felt even more disconnected from the life I had left behind.

In this state of limbo, I decided to stay for another week. I knew I needed to continue to step away from the known and venture deeper into the unknown. I was standing at the epicenter of a storm where the chaos of healing collided with the profound pain of self-discovery.

When my time in Rythmia ended, I was scared. I couldn't look at men without wondering if they were abusing their kids.

I needed a man, who felt safe, to hold my hand and tell me everything would be alright. I reached out to friends I felt safe with in search of comfort. But no one was there for me.

Realizing that I was alone during such a vulnerable time was heart-wrenching. It saddened me deeply, leaving a profound ache in my heart.

However, after all the pain I had endured those weeks, it felt like no other pain could truly touch me.

Newfound Clarity

I decided to talk to my family and flew back home. It wasn't fear of their reaction that held me back initially; it was the immense weight of the truth I had to share.

I sat down with my mom and my sister Karina first. As I spoke with tears rolling down my face, I could see the devastation in their eyes.

My heart broke witnessing their pain, yet I noticed a flicker of understanding in the midst of it. The light of clarity illuminated their faces as I shared my experiences with them.

What I told them answered many questions that had plagued them for years regarding our history, my father, my behaviors, and my middle sister's behaviors.

Later I spoke with my half-sister, Monica. She arrived in our lives right before my eldest brother's death.

It is often complex to navigate the arrival of a new sibling. We all had our challenges. Yet, she was very understanding when we spoke, and we have a closer friendship now than before.

About a year later, I spoke with my middle sister, Evelyn. She is working through new painful questions that came up for her.

My brother Julio has also been a great support. He is always there for us girls.

I often wonder what my deceased brother Robert, with all his hidden traumas and pains, would have had to say on the matter.

Healing as a Family

My healing journey not only brought me closer to myself, but it also brought our family closer together, offering a deeper comprehension of the struggles we had faced as individuals and as a unit.

Through my sharing, we embarked on a healing journey as a family. The process is ongoing and it involves acknowledging the wounds and traumas we carry collectively and individually and finding the strength to face them together.

Our family dynamics began to shift. The healing journey helps us to communicate more openly. We now have a deeper level of empathy and compassion among us and with others. The truth allowed us to approach our past with greater understanding and acceptance.

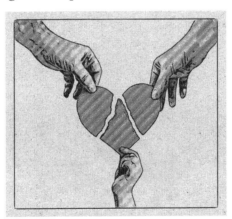

Your Family

I hope my family's journey sparks a glimmer of hope within you. Family healing is a profound and transformative process that requires each member's courage, vulnerability, and dedication. There might be challenges along the way, but I assure you, the effort is worth it.

Not all families are open or ready to embark on a healing journey together, and that's okay. Each family is unique, and healing takes time and willingness from all involved. Even if your family isn't open to the process, you can still do your part in your own healing and growth.

By acknowledging and working through your wounds and traumas, you can break free from old patterns and create a positive ripple effect within your family and beyond. I will talk about this ripple effect later in the book.

My Quest

A passion is born when you stumble upon something that truly excites you. That newfound passion becomes a healthy obsession, the driving force that propels you toward your life's purpose. It fuels your journey and adds meaning to every step you take.

When I returned from Costa Rica, I went on a quest for knowledge. Until then, I had achieved and done many things in my life. Yet, I felt I needed a purpose; I was not passionate about anything.

The deeper I dove into my own experiences, the more passionate I became about studying all aspects of trauma. How it affects society as a whole. And how traumatic memories are stored in the brain and the body.

How trauma, when unhealed, can be a silent killer of joy in a person's life. And how adversities can be transmuted into valuable lessons with the help of psychedelics and alternative treatments.

Eckhart Tolle writes, "The secret of life is to die before you die." I died and was reborn the night of my third Ayahuasca treatment. I was free to rebuild myself with a foundation of past experiences and many new healthy coping mechanisms.

Until you come face to face with excruciating adversity, it's impossible to know, with absolute certainty, how you would react. The months following my discovery showed me that my soul is a warrior soul.

PART 3
Below the Surface

*"The more I learn, the more I realize
how much I don't know."*

– Albert Einstein

This portion of the book is of immense importance.
It takes a momentary detour from the main narrative. The
next six chapters touch on the intricate interplay of trauma,
memories, psychedelics, and science.

Part Three will explore the following questions:

- How does the brain store memories?
- Why does the brain hide memories? How are memories
  recovered?
- Can your mind be hiding memories?
- Why is there stigma and silence surrounding
  unremembered trauma?
- What are some of the stigmas associated with
  psychedelics?
- Which substances are being used for trauma healing?
- Why are psychedelic medicines illegal?
- How do psychedelics offer an accelerated path to
  healing?
- What are some of the recommendations and dangers
  to be aware of when embarking on any alternative
  medicine treatment?
- What can you expect during a treatment or a ceremony?

- How are memories of trauma transmitted through generations?
- What questions must you ask if hidden memories come up during your own treatment?

It is vital you explore this section, as the final part of the book will expand on the concepts I present here.

Some of you might be eager to continue reading the narrative story at the heart of this memoir. If you cannot resist the anticipation, feel free to skip ahead to the fourth and last part. Yet, I recommend that you return to this section after you've finished the story, as it holds valuable insights to complement the journey.

CHAPTER 25
Trauma and Memory

"The human brain is the most extraordinary and complex object in the known universe."

– David Eagleman

Picture life as a cup of water. Imagine trauma as drops of different color dye. Initially, when the dye is dropped into the water, it dissolves and releases little dye molecules into the solution.

These molecules are constantly moving, and soon the entire solution turns the color of the dye. For example, if my dye is blue and your dye is yellow, then my cup of water ends up tainted by my blue dye just as much as your cup of water ends up tainted by your yellow dye.

Similarly, your life becomes tainted by trauma and its consequences just as much as mine. Even traumatic experiences that may seem small or insignificant affect how you perceive the world around you, your opinion of yourself, and of others later in life.

Your dye and my dye are as different as our fingerprints. The dyes might be emotional neglect by a parent, physical abuse by a sibling, molestation by a cousin, verbal abuse by a peer, or domestic violence, among others. The nature or the perceived severity of the traumas is not the key.

How you experience and process the emotions that arise as a consequence of those traumas determines how pervasive and severe the effects are.

The Brain as an Apple

Trauma alters the brain's structure and functioning. The areas responsible for emotional regulation, memory processing, and the stress response system are most affected. I will explain the science behind this using a few simple examples.

Imagine the brain as an apple. Just as an apple has different parts, your brain has various sections, each with unique functions.

The stem of the apple represents the reptilian brain, the oldest and most primitive part of your brain. It controls essential functions for your survival, like regulating your heartbeat, breathing, and body temperature.

Just as the stem connects the apple to its source, the reptilian brain connects you to your basic instincts and ensures your body functions properly.

Moving to the core of the apple, you find the emotional brain. This part of your brain includes structures like the amygdala and hippocampus. The amygdala is responsible for processing and regulating your emotions, especially fear and anxiety. This area activates the fight or flight response when you face a threat.

When new information comes in or you experience a new event, the hippocampus forms new memories. Short-term memories go through a process called consolidation. They get transferred from the hippocampus onto other brain areas for long-term storage.

The hippocampus organizes the details of the experiences, including context, time, and space in which the events occurred. It also records the emotions you felt during the experience.

It is important to note that the emotional brain communicates with feelings and emotions, not with words. These feelings and emotions influence your reactions and shape your perceptions of the world.

Lastly, you have the flesh on the front of the apple, which can be compared to your brain's frontal lobe. The frontal lobe is the outermost part of the brain and is involved in higher-level thinking processes. It is often called the rational brain. It allows you to make decisions, solve problems, plan for the future, and control your behavior.

Just as the flesh of the apple surrounds and protects the core, the frontal lobe acts as a shield, guiding your actions and helping you navigate the complexities of life. This is where your feelings and emotions are converted into a narrative.

The Fabric of Your Memories

During regular life episodes, all of the parts of the brain work together in harmony. An external stimulus is received and converted, so it can be processed and stored. It gets consolidated and integrated into the neural networks.

Let's compare the storing and retrieval of a memory to the folding and storing of a fabric.

Imagine you have a fabric that you want to store. When you first get the fabric, you carefully fold it up and put it away in a drawer. This is like storing a regular memory in your brain. Your brain organizes the memory and puts it away for safekeeping until you need to retrieve it later.

When you want to retrieve a regular memory, it's like taking the fabric out of the drawer and unfolding it. You can see the fabric in its original form, just how you stored it.

Similarly, when you retrieve a regular memory, your brain brings it back into your awareness, and you can remember the details of the memory as it happened.

A Special Fabric

Scientists explain that during a traumatic episode, the amygdala goes into overdrive (heightened fear response). And the activity in the rational brain and hippocampus decreases. During traumatic experiences, memory storage gets affected in several ways. Trauma changes the processes of encoding, consolidating, and retrieving memories.

This is such a key point that I will write it again: Traumatic memories are not encoded, consolidated, stored, or retrieved in the same way as non-traumatic memories.

Let's use the same fabric example to describe what happens in the brain during a traumatic episode.

Imagine you have a special fabric that you want to store. This fabric has unique patterns and textures. When you put that fabric away in the drawer, something happens. The fabric gets all wrinkled and tangled in a way that's different from how you first folded it. This is similar to how a traumatic memory is stored in your brain.

When you try to retrieve it, the fabric doesn't unfold how you originally folded it. It might be twisted, wrinkled, or even torn. Similarly, when you retrieve a traumatic memory, it may not come back in the same way it was stored. The memory can feel fragmented, incomplete, or intense. It often triggers strong emotions.

This doesn't mean that the memory is wrong or false. It's just that the highly emotional nature of the traumatic experience affected how the memory was stored and retrieved. So, just like the fabric looks different when you unfold it after being stored in a unique way, traumatic memories are retrieved in a way that feels different from regular memories.

People who might have experienced traumatic events in their childhood often have difficulty recalling good memories from that time.

Three of the most common explanations for this phenomenon are:

- **Limited Mental Resources:** When suffering trauma, the brain has no resources left to neatly fold and store the regular fabric or the good memories the person experiences.

  Just as shoving a large piece of special fabric into the back of a drawer takes up space. Hiding a traumatic memory and ensuring it stays hidden takes up a lot of mental space and energy. The brain's coping mechanisms prioritize suppressing distressing memories rather than storing good memories.

- **Perpetual High-Alert State:** When many traumatic memories need to be stored, the brain learns to stay in a perpetual high-alert state. The brain feels like a baby gazelle, and it perceives anything nearby as a hungry leopard. This constant state of vigilance can persist even during non-threatening moments, affecting the brain's ability to access and recall pleasant memories.

- **Fear of Unintended Trauma Recall:** The psyche won't risk unfolding a special fabric or traumatic memory by mistake. Regular fabrics can get tangled up with special fabrics. The brain fears the act of recalling a good memory that is closely related to a traumatic event could trigger traumatic memories to come back to conscious awareness. The brain ensures your survival; recalling traumatic memories feels like death. It must be avoided at all costs.

These mechanisms of self-preservation explained my lack of good childhood memories.

Vivid Memories and PTSD

In some cases, traumatic memories are stored as vivid and distressing recollections. These memories are typically associated with intense emotions and detailed sensory impressions.

Single traumatic events, such as natural disasters, accidents, or one-time instances of physical or sexual assault, are often stored and recalled in this way.

There are striking similarities between how traumatic memories from war and traumatic memories from childhood are stored in the brain. For example, a child who endured a severe physical assault and a soldier who faced a disturbing combat-related incident might store and recall memories vividly and intensely.

Soldiers and children exposed to isolated traumatic events that overwhelmed their ability to cope and process their experiences often develop PTSD (Post-Traumatic Stress Disorder).

The memories that lead to suffering from PTSD can come to the surface as distressing flashbacks, nightmares, intrusive thoughts, emotional numbness, and hypervigilance.

These memories often contain intense emotions, fear, and a sense of helplessness associated with the traumatic event. They can be triggered by reminders of the original trauma, such as sights, sounds, smells, or situations reminiscent of the war or the traumatic episode.

The symptoms of PTSD typically persist for at least one month and can last for months or even years if left untreated. While some individuals may experience a partial or complete remission of symptoms over time, others may struggle with ongoing symptoms.

No Vivid Recollection

In other cases, a person goes through life without vivid recollections or distressing flashbacks. Perhaps it makes you wonder: How can that person heal a wound they don't know exists? How can they answer questions they don't know to ask?

My mind stored my traumatic memories in this much more hidden way, but neither my subconscious nor my body forgot. The next chapter explains the science behind that defense mechanism.

CHAPTER 26
Beyond Recall

"Our bodies remember trauma, even if our minds don't."

– Bessel Van der Kolk

With its remarkable complexity, the human brain can be both a fortress and a vulnerable sanctuary. It safeguards you from the full weight of your pain yet inadvertently sacrifices cherished memories.

I was just three years old when the abuse began. It continued until my father died when I was 16 years old.

When my eldest brother got ill, mom was away from the house, caring for him. I slept in my mom's bed at home, often next to my dad. I used something called dissociation as a coping mechanism, in order to survive.

Forgetting memories typically occurs when certain information or experiences become inaccessible or fade over time. This could be due to various factors, such as a lack of reinforcement or retrieval cues, interference from other memories, or neurological conditions affecting memory retention. On the other hand, traumatic dissociation is a psychological defense mechanism.

Dissociation and C-PTSD

Dissociation generally develops in response to prolonged or repeated trauma, such as ongoing childhood abuse, long episodes of domestic violence, prolonged neglect, long combat situations, or captivity.

Dissociation often goes hand in hand with another diagnosis that plagues soldiers and trauma survivors called C-PTSD (Complex Post-Traumatic Stress Disorder). In 2020, the World Health Organization (WHO) introduced C-PTSD as a new diagnostic category. This move acknowledged the complex interplay of trauma-related symptoms that extend beyond the scope of traditional Post-Traumatic Stress Disorder (PTSD) criteria.

While PTSD can develop following isolated traumatic events, C-PTSD is a condition resulting from prolonged and repeated trauma. Common dissociative experiences in individuals with C-PTSD may include:

- **Dissociative Amnesia:** Gaps in memory or an inability to recall certain aspects of the traumatic events or significant periods of your life.
- **Depersonalization:** Feeling detached from your body or like an outside observer of your thoughts and actions.
- **Derealization:** Sensing that the world around you is unreal, dreamlike, or distant.
- **Identity Confusion:** Struggling to have a stable and coherent sense of self, often experiencing changes in identity or self-perception.
- **Emotional Numbing:** Feeling emotionally detached or having limited access to feelings to shield yourself from overwhelming emotions.
- **Dissociative Trance:** Periods of spacing out or losing track of time, often during stressful or triggering situations.

Symptoms of dissociation and C-PTSD may include difficulties in emotional regulation, persistent feelings of shame or guilt, disturbances in self-identity, difficulties in forming and maintaining relationships, chronic feelings of emptiness or hopelessness, and a sense of being trapped or unable to escape the traumatic memories.

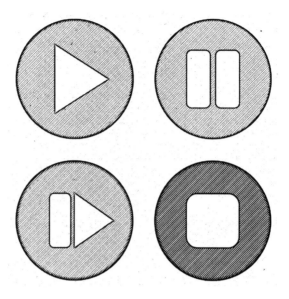

Pausing and Forwarding

Trauma creates intense emotional disruptions. Peter Levine explains in his book, *In An Unspoken Voice*, that "when such disruptions fail to be fully integrated, the components of that experience become fragmented into isolated sensations, images, and emotions. This kind of splitting apart occurs when the enormity, intensity, suddenness, or duration of what happened cannot be defended against, coped with, or digested. Personal vulnerability, such as age, genetics and gender also account for this psychic implosion."

Imagine your life as a movie, where most of the time, everything flows smoothly, and you feel connected to the story and characters. A traumatic event is like a jarring scene in the movie that overwhelms you. Dissociation is like hitting the pause button or even fast-forwarding through that part of the movie.

The brain's goal is to shield you from the intense emotions tied to the trauma by creating a separation between yourself and the memory of the event.

In the aftermath of a traumatic event, your memory of the scene may be unclear and fragmented, like watching a blurred version of the movie.

Dissociation is a common way to store traumatic memories when the trauma is experienced during early childhood, as the child's brain and coping mechanisms are still forming.

My Dissociation

Throughout my childhood, I pressed the fast-forward and pause buttons many times to cope with the overwhelming experiences I endured.

As a little girl, I didn't yet have words in my vocabulary to express what was happening. I also lacked the knowledge to understand it.

My father, who was my primary caregiver, engaged in behavior that triggered the fear center in my brain. When he did, fear would take over, and I would become powerless, scared, and confused.

My survival instinct kicked, and a dissociative bubble formed. I felt like the events were happening outside of my bubble. In my bubble, I was safe, and the emotions were not so intense.

As I grew older and the severity of the events escalated, I felt a split in my mind: I could watch myself and observe the situation without being part of it. I formed two separate realities. One was a normal reality, and the other was a secret reality. My brain made that secret reality seem so distant that, for years, it was as if it didn't happen.

Imagine you are watching your favorite movie for the seventh time. Even if you sometimes mute it or take bathroom breaks, you still know what's happening in the movie. The plot is ingrained in your mind. Watching my mental screen during my treatment in Costa Rica felt just like that. The images on the screen were blurry. Yet, I knew exactly what the movie was about.

My nervous system recalled the memories as intense feelings and emotions accompanied by deep inner knowing and familiarity.

Understanding how my brain protected me made me realize that healing is not just about retrieving the lost pieces of the movie but also about understanding the emotions and inner knowing that remains.

I had to acknowledge the impact of those traumatic scenes and gradually piece together the puzzle pieces of my life with compassion and self-awareness. I had to honor my experiences, no matter how fragmented and disturbing, so I could heal and grow stronger from within.

Is Your Brain Protecting You?

As you reflect on my journey and how my brain protected me, consider the possibility that your brain might have done something similar for you. Your mind is intricate and mysterious, capable of shielding you from painful memories or emotions until you are courageous enough to face them.

There are various indications or possible clues that could point to hidden trauma. These are not absolute; they are simply guidelines. Ask yourself:

1. **Unexplained emotional reactions:** Do I find myself experiencing intense emotional responses that feel overwhelming and out of proportion to the situation I might be going through? Or do I hold beliefs that make no rational sense?

2. **Chronic physical symptoms:** Have I been dealing with persistent physical ailments such as autoimmune diseases, chronic headaches, stomachaches, or unexplained pain, even when there's no clear medical explanation?

3. **Coping mechanisms:** Do I notice that I rely on unhealthy coping mechanisms, such as substance abuse or excessive work, to escape from emotional pain?

4. **Difficulty forming or maintaining relationships:** Do I struggle to build and sustain meaningful connections with others due to trust issues or fear of getting hurt?

5. **Avoidance and emotional detachment:** Have I been avoiding certain places, people, or situations that might trigger distressing memories, and do I sometimes feel emotionally detached as a way to protect myself?

6. **Intrusive thoughts or nightmares:** Do I experience distressing memories or nightmares I can't quite explain that impact my sleep or ability to focus?

7. **Low self-esteem and self-worth:** Do I often battle feelings of inadequacy, shame, or self-blame, possibly stemming from past experiences?

8. **Anxiety and hypervigilance:** Have I been living in a state of constant alertness and heightened sensitivity, always on the lookout for potential threats?

9. **Difficulty regulating emotions:** Do I find it challenging to manage my emotions, leading to outbursts of anger, sadness, or feeling emotionally numb?

10. **Memory gaps or fragmented memories:** Have I noticed gaps in my memories or trouble recalling specific events from my past?

Become Curious

Remember, these signs can indicate hidden trauma but can also be connected to other factors. If some of those questions resonate with you, exploring your feelings and experiences with the guidance of a qualified mental health professional who can offer support may be worthwhile.

I explored the root of these questions with the help of ayahuasca and other psychedelics. I will describe later how each treatment and substance helped me change my life.

As you embark on your own explorations, follow any path that feels right. Embracing curiosity and self-compassion, you can gently explore the fragments of your life's puzzle and embark on your healing journey.

The notion that your brain can hide traumatic memories might be new to you. However, these scientific discoveries have been part of psychological literature for decades. In the next chapter, I dive into some of the reasons why this vital concept is not as widely known as it should be.

Hidden Memories

CHAPTER 27
Walls of Secrecy

"If you are neutral in situations of injustice, you have chosen the side of the oppressor."

– Archbishop Desmond Tutu

The consequences of trauma are like a thick fog that seems to always be there, stationed on top of millions of people's heads.

These people look at the weather forecast for guidance, but they get even more confused because the weatherman says it is sunny. Yet, it does not look sunny to them. So, they blame themselves, take prescription medications, drink alcohol, and do drugs. But none of that makes their life warm and bright.

Sometimes, they catch glimpses of the sun. It appears briefly when they have a breakthrough in therapy. When they meet the love of their lives. When they buy a puppy or when they birth a child. And those glimpses become enough. More often than not, people go through life right up to their last days, not ever knowing why the fog was always there.

Regrettably, for far too long, the profound effects of trauma remained shrouded in darkness. However, the tides are turning, and change is on the horizon. In this transformative era, not only are people breaking free from the fog, but studies on trauma are also being more widely distributed, and books are speaking more openly about it.

Mental Parasites

Bessel A. Van der Kolk, M.D. is a renowned psychiatrist and expert in trauma and post-traumatic stress disorder (PTSD). He gives an excellent historical overview of trauma-related studies in his book *The Body Keeps the Score: Brain, Mind, and Body in the Healing of Trauma.*

The study of trauma and how the human brain stores memories dates back to the late nineteenth century. Scientists such as Pierre Janet, Jean Martin Charcot, and Sigmund Freud were pioneers in this field during the 1880s and beyond.

They referred to traumatic memories as "pathogenic secrets" or "mental parasites," recognizing that these memories persistently intruded into consciousness, trapping individuals in an unending cycle of existential horror.

Janet, in particular, was the first to propose that traumatic memories are stored differently, coining the term "dissociation" to describe the coping mechanism patients used to disconnect from overwhelming or distressing experiences.

He observed that those who suffered from dissociation became "attached to an insurmountable obstacle," losing their ability to assimilate new experiences. He predicted their personal and professional lives would suffer if they didn't address their forgotten traumas.

During the late nineteenth century, hysteria was considered a medical condition primarily associated with women. It encompassed a range of physical and emotional symptoms, including fainting, sadness, anger, and loss of bodily control. However, studies during that period began shedding light on the true nature of hysteria.

In 1893, Freud and his mentor wrote a paper positing that "Hysterics suffer mainly from reminiscences." They believed hysteria was caused by unconscious thoughts and emotions hidden from conscious awareness.

They wrote: "These experiences are completely absent from the patient's memory when they are in a normal psychical state or are only present in a highly summary form."

Seduction of a Child

Freud's groundbreaking work introduced the idea of the mind's divided levels of consciousness, where specific thoughts and feelings remained hidden or repressed.

I was shocked when I read what Freud boldly proclaimed in 1896. He said, "The ultimate cause of hysteria is always the seduction of a child by an adult."

I wondered why this elite scientist, viewed as the founder of psychoanalysis, was not known for these studies.

Dr. Bessel Van der Kolk answered my question in his book: "Faced with his own evidence of an epidemic of abuse in the best families of Vienna-one, he noted, that implicated his own father-he quickly began to retreat." Freud psychoanalysis studies changed course after that.

The seeds of trauma and abuse find fertile ground to grow and thrive in the caverns of silence and stigma.

Avalanche of Trauma

Childhood abuse (verbal, physical, and sexual) has been deemed one of the largest, if not the largest, epidemic that plagues the world. The CDC (Centers for Disease Control and Prevention) reports in 2023 that "at least, 1 in 7 children have experienced child abuse or neglect in the past year in the United States. This is likely an underestimate because many cases are unreported."

If we were to add to the reported number the cases that never get reported due to fear or dissociation, we end up with an astronomical number of abused and neglected children.

Pause for a moment and let the gravity of those numbers sink in: one child out of every seven is abused or neglected in the USA alone.

The prevalence of childhood abuse and neglect is staggering, with countless children enduring pain and suffering behind closed doors all over the world. It's a silent epidemic that leaves scars that last a lifetime.

These children will carry the consequences of the abuse and neglect into adulthood. And in many cases, they will treat their children the same way they were treated. Perpetuating an ever-expanding snowball of suffering. Society a whole is being swept away by an avalanche of trauma.

Each of us plays a role in bringing awareness to the staggering scale of abuse and neglect. We can no longer turn a blind eye to the suffering of these children.

As a society, we must join hands to break this cycle, offering support, empathy, and resources to those in need. Together, we can create a ripple effect of healing, gifting the generations to come with a brighter and more hopeful future.

A Shameful Stain

From stifling the voices of victims to shielding the abuser from accountability, the walls of secrecy become the fortress that upholds the cycle of abuses and traumas.

Perhaps some of you remember the trials against the Catholic church during the 1980s and 1990s. The allegations involved priests, bishops, and other clergy members engaging in sexual misconduct, particularly with minors. These cases often included accusations of molestation, rape, and other sexual exploitation.

The public became outraged as the number of allegations increased. The media became interested, and demands for accountability started to show up everywhere.

Survivors of abuse came forward to share their experiences, and law enforcement agencies, independent organizations, and the church itself initiated investigations.

These incidents started to shed light onto childhood's traumatic memories being remembered later in life.

Unfortunately, instead of addressing these issues head-on, the church used legal and administrative tactics to impede investigations or to protect accused priests, such as settling cases out of court with non-disclosure agreements.

The impact of questioning and dismissing survivors' experiences left the survivors grappling with self-doubt, internal conflicts, and fear of speaking out. This skepticism towards abuse allegations silenced survivors and perpetuated a dangerous culture of disbelief.

If the major and widespread allegations had been taken seriously during those high-profile trials, abusers would have thought twice before engaging in future abuse. And abused adults would have come forward more readily.

This chapter in the history of the Catholic Church during the 1980s and 1990s stands as a shameful and deeply troubling stain on both the religious and legal systems of the United States.

Our collective responsibility is to learn from this and ensure that such injustices are never allowed to occur again. Protection of the innocent must always take precedence over the power and financial reach of the parties involved.

Domino Effect

In a haunting parallel, the medical community also discredited traumatized soldiers.

The medical community didn't understand why soldiers returned home with symptoms like nightmares, flashbacks, anxiety, and difficulty coping with daily life. The doctors didn't know what caused or how to treat those symptoms. Some experts often dismissed them as signs of weakness or hinted the soldiers were faking them.

Other doctors focused more on the soldier's physical injuries, believing that the cause of the symptoms was physical trauma or damage to the nervous system.

In recent times, a transformative shift has begun to emerge. The once-shrouded reality of veterans' pain is now being brought to light. More awareness surrounds the profound emotional and psychological effects of war.

However, it is clear that more needs to be done since, according to the 2019 USA survey on drug and health, 3.9 million veterans had a mental illness and/or substance use disorder. The 2020 survey showed that number had increased to 5.2 million.

These men and women are suffering from the effects of trauma, and they are bringing those effects home to their families. Their young children are growing up in an environment that might not be optimal for their development. These children might also be parents one day. It's a domino effect that has no end in sight unless something changes.

Are you or someone you know a veteran who might be silently suffering from the effects of trauma? Or perhaps you are a family member, a child, or a parent who has witnessed the aftermath of trauma in your loved ones. The different healing alternatives I mention later in the book prove to be revolutionary in helping soldiers and their families.

Quick Fixes

You have likely heard of people being diagnosed with conditions like depression, anxiety, bipolar illness, PTSD, or ADHD, but did you know that these diagnoses are often rooted in trauma?

Dr. Gabor Maté, sheds light on this connection and suggests that these diagnoses are often manifestations of trauma, not standalone conditions.

He explains, "The problem in the medical world is that we diagnose somebody and we think that is the explanation. He's behaving that way because he is psychotic. She's behaving that way because she has ADHD. Nobody has ADHD, nobody has psychosis - these are processes within the individual. It's not a thing that you have. This is a process that expresses your life experience. It has meaning in every single case."

Medications are commonly prescribed to treat these conditions. But they don't address the underlying root causes. They focus on symptom suppression which can lead to a host of additional side effects.

Have you ever felt overwhelmed and confused by the laundry list of potential side effects mentioned in drug commercials or in the lengthy booklets accompanying medications? You are not alone.

Society can shift its focus from symptom suppression to true healing by exploring alternative approaches that honor the complexity of trauma and prioritize holistic well-being.

Research on the use of psychedelics for treating PTSD and C-PTSD in soldiers and trauma victims has shown promising results. Unfortunately, red tape prevents these treatments from being readily available for those in need.

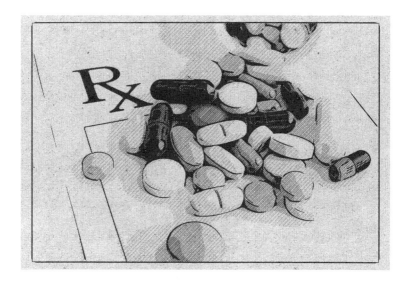

Your Reflections

One must question if some of the red tape that stops psychedelics and plant medicine from being legalized is being bought by the industries that would be more affected by their legalization. Industries that prioritize profit over health, such as the pharmaceutical, alcohol and tobacco industries.

These billion-dollar industries would lose immense amounts of money if people started to be more interested in discovering and healing from what has happened to them rather than trying to deal with what is wrong with them.

Have you ever wondered how many lives could have been positively transformed, and perhaps saved if psychedelic therapies had been accessible to them?

Think about the people in your life, your friends, family, or even yourself, who may be struggling with mental health issues or the lingering effects of trauma. Could psychedelics make a difference in your life?

Each day that passes without progress feels like an eternity for those in need as they continue to battle their inner demons, hoping for a breakthrough.

Dismantling the Red Tape

Dismantling the red tape surrounding alternative therapies and shifting away from industries that profit from addiction and suffering would open doors to hope and possibility.

It would create space for innovative treatments, like psychedelics, to be explored for their potential to heal deep-rooted traumas. By prioritizing true healing, you can help pave the way for a future where mental health is treated with the depth and sensitivity it deserves.

Your awareness and engagement in this issue makes a significant difference and offers hope to those still searching for relief.

The next chapter explores alternative treatments and the potential transformative power of psychedelics in trauma healing.

CHAPTER 28
Not Your Typical Drug

"The art of medicine consists in amusing the patient, while nature cures the disease."

– Voltaire

Trauma is far more than a conventional disease; it represents a profound experience of dis-ease and dis-order within the very core of your being. Unfelt emotions are at the origin of trauma.

Unfelt emotions are those you experience during a traumatic episode that you don't fully process or express.

The overwhelming intensity of the emotions, your age, or circumstances surrounding the trauma determines if you suppress and disconnect from your emotions temporarily or permanently.

These unfelt emotions remain trapped within you, impacting your psyche and plaguing you with consequences.

In his support of this belief, Sigmund Freud divided trauma healing into two essential components: the "talking cure" and the "arousal of the accompanying effect."

The talking cure involves verbally expressing your thoughts and feelings, which provides insight into your unconscious mind and underlying psychological struggles.

However, the key to healing seems to be in the second component: the feeling and processing of the accompanying emotions tied to the recalled traumatic memories.

Did it Work for You?

Have you ever experienced the power of the talking cure? Perhaps you've sat in a psychiatrist or psychologist's office, or maybe you talked to a friend. Verbally expressing your innermost feelings can be a profoundly transformative experience. Maybe the complexities of your life demanded an ongoing exploration, and you found yourself returning week after week, yearning for further insights and healing.

Take a moment to ponder if you felt you could navigate through your emotions, even when they were painful or uncomfortable. Did you find the courage to process and release the trauma attached to them? Or did you feel that you needed more support?

If after talking through it, you still display patterns or behaviors you can't explain or are grappling with unproductive emotions you can't shake, consider continuing your healing exploration.

Remember, healing is a multifaceted journey with no one-size-fits-all approach. Being open to alternative therapies, such as psychedelics, can be a valuable addition to your healing toolkit. These approaches are not a replacement for traditional therapy or other forms of support. Instead, they offer a unique and complementary way to navigate your journey.

Accelerated Path to Healing

Recognizing that trauma can be most effectively healed when you can process and release emotions tied to traumatic memories illuminates the extraordinary healing potential of treatments involving psychedelics and plant medicines.

Imagine embarking on a therapeutic journey where you compress the progress you would typically make over years of traditional therapy into brief and intense emotional explorations.

Psychedelics help you dive into the depth of your psyche in an accelerated way. During treatments you can confront emotions that have long remained buried. And perhaps, just like me, you might discover complex hidden trauma that holds the key to your metamorphosis.

Dissolving Barriers

The magic of psychedelics and plant medicines lies in their ability to create a unique and heightened state of consciousness. Within this altered state, the barriers that once shielded you from your emotions begin to dissolve. You're given access to the innermost chambers of your soul, where the seeds of trauma were sown.

During my emotional exploration, I experienced moments of catharsis, where long-held burdens were finally lifted. The weight of past pain, fear, and guilt began to dissipate, and a newfound sense of clarity and understanding emerged.

These substances helped me connect with my emotions in a way I had never experienced before. They could do the same for you but remember that, ultimately, it is your call. Your responsibility is to find what resonates with you, feels safe, and aligns with your values and goals.

Challenging Your Assumptions

Psychedelics have been unfairly associated with counterculture and recreational use, leading to widespread misconceptions and negative perceptions. Let's explore some common stigmas and fears surrounding psychedelics to see if you hold any of these beliefs:

Stigma: Psychedelics are just recreational party drugs and have no therapeutic value.

Stigma-buster: Have you considered looking beyond the association of psychedelics with counterculture and recreational use to uncover their hidden potential in therapeutic settings? Were you aware of the recent rekindling of interest in their use for mental health issues?

Stigma: Psychedelics are dangerous and can cause permanent mental damage.

Stigma-buster: What if your lack of understanding of psychedelics is preventing you from discovering groundbreaking therapeutic applications? Did you know that when used responsibly and under proper guidance, psychedelics can be safer than many prescription drugs?

Stigma: Psychedelic users are reckless. Only "hippies" use them.

Stigma-buster: Are your stereotypes preventing you from recognizing the diversity of individuals who explore these substances for various reasons, including personal growth and mental health? Did you know that veterans are one of the main groups treated with psychedelic-assisted therapies?

Stigma: Psychedelics have a high potential for addiction.

Stigma-buster: Are your preconceived notions about addiction and long-term effects preventing you from exploring a new paradigm of mental health care? Did you know many psychedelics are less addictive than alcohol or cigarettes?

Stigma: The spiritual experiences induced by psychedelics are not genuine; they are just hallucinations.

Stigma-buster: Are you open to exploring the scientific evidence that suggests psychedelic experiences bear genuine and profound insights into the nature of consciousness and the human mind?

Your Thoughts on Drug Policies

Most psychedelic substances are illegal. Powerful people with financial interests resist change and prevent legalization. In the USA, they are classified as Schedule I or controlled substances.

Consider the paradoxical classification of the substances as "Schedule I" in the United States, which designates them as having no accepted medical use. This classification implies that these substances provide no medicinal value, despite scientific evidence pointing to the contrary.

In light of the growing body of research supporting the therapeutic potential of these substances, can you reconcile the discrepancy between their proven medical benefits and their continued classification as having no accepted medical use? How does this knowledge impact your perception of drug policies and their alignment with scientific evidence? Ponder on the following points:

- **Discrepancy Between Policy and Research:**
  Scientific evidence demonstrates the therapeutic benefits of certain substances, yet they remain classified as having no medical use. This calls into question the extent to which drug policies are informed by scientific findings or influenced by monetary interests.

- **Barriers to Research:**
  The Schedule I classification creates barriers to further research on these substances, making it difficult for scientists to conduct studies to explore their potential

medical applications. This limitation in research hinders the development of potentially valuable treatments.

- **Impact on Patients:**
  Patients who could potentially benefit from these substances for medical conditions may face limited or no access to effective treatments due to their Schedule I status.

- **Potential for Legal Consequences:**
  Individuals who use these substances for medical purposes in states or countries where they are not legalized may face legal consequences, even if their use is supported by scientific evidence and medical professionals.

In summary, the Schedule I classification of substances with known medical potential challenges the alignment of drug policies with scientific evidence. It highlights the need for a more evidence-based approach to drug policy formulation, one that considers the medical benefits and risks associated with these substances while also prioritizing the well-being of patients and the broader public health.

Let's take a closer look at some of these substances:

Plant medicines:

1. **Magic Mushrooms and Ayahuasca.**
   Psilocybin is a naturally occurring psychedelic compound found in what is commonly known as "magic mushrooms." It was "discovered" by science in the 50s. Yet, indigenous cultures have used

mushrooms containing psilocybin for spiritual and healing purposes for thousands of years.

The active compounds of ayahuasca and psilocybin affect the body differently when ingested. Yet, their effect on the brain is similar.

Think back to the example I presented in Chapter 25 that compares memories to a fabric. With psilocybin and ayahuasca, it's as if the special fabric in the drawer is being unfolded in a magical way, allowing you to see glimpses of the memories stored within.

The psychedelic experience can bring forth vivid imagery, sensory hallucinations, heightened emotions, and introspective insights. It may enable you to explore traumatic memories and their associated feelings from a different perspective.

2. **San Pedro and Peyote.**

San Pedro is a cacti native to the Andean region of South America. It has been used for centuries by indigenous cultures, particularly in Peru and Ecuador, for spiritual and healing purposes. It is also known as, huachuma cactus.

It contains various alkaloids, including mescaline, responsible for its hallucinogenic effects. Mescaline is also the psychoactive compound contained in peyote. Peyote cacti are native to the southwestern regions of the United States and northern Mexico.

In traditional practices, San Pedro and peyote often induce altered states of consciousness, facilitate spiritual connection, and promote healing and introspection.

Compared to ayahuasca, San Pedro and peyote are often less intense and more gradual. Users may experience visual distortions, enhanced sensory perception, and emotional insights.

The effects of mescaline tend to be more prolonged. A treatment can last 12 hours or more, often allowing for a gentler exploration of the inner psyche.

Imagine the fabric that holds the traumatic memory being tucked away in the drawer, peyote and San Pedro provide a gentle nudge, encouraging you to unfold the fabric and start exploring its contents. Similarly to psilocybin and ayahuasca, they facilitate a sense of connectedness and openness, allowing you to approach challenging memories with curiosity and compassion.

Man-made Substances:
1. **MDMA.**

MDMA (sometimes called ecstasy or Molly) is a synthetic psychoactive substance. It is classified as an empathogen and stimulant because it enhances feelings of empathy, emotional openness, and euphoria.

In the book *A Dose of Hope*, Dan Engle explains that during MDMA therapy, the amygdala, which is the brain's fear center, relaxes. The substance also helps achieve higher self-awareness in the observation part of the brain (that same rational brain that gets shut down during a traumatic episode).

Contrary to the disconnection that happens during the formation of traumatic memories, MDMA enhances the connection between the rational brain and the hippocampus (where memories are formed, processed, and consolidated).

This incredible combination allows the memories stored deep in the brain to be processed and reorganized without the same intensity of fear felt when the events happened. There is even more blood flowing into the memory and emotional areas of the brain.

Imagine you have the fabric that holds the difficult memory stored in a very deep drawer. MDMA is a substance that can help you feel more open and connected. It gently opens that drawer. It creates a safe and supportive environment where you can begin to unfold the fabric and explore its contents.

With the help of MDMA, you may experience a sense of emotional release and insight.

2. LSD.

LSD (lysergic acid diethylamide) is a powerful psychedelic substance. It is derived from a fungus called ergot and was first synthesized in a laboratory in 1938.

However, according to some historians and researchers, the discovery of ergot in ancient grain supplies and the historical use of psychoactive substances for spiritual and religious reasons provide evidence that people in ancient Greece and Egypt might have used Ergot to achieve altered states of consciousness.

LSD is known for its mind-altering effects, including hallucinations, altered perceptions of time and space, and profound changes in thought patterns and emotions.

LSD can temporarily reduce the activity of the amygdala, helping to calm down the fear response and create a sense of safety during therapy. It can also increase the connectivity and communication between different brain regions, including the hippocampus, which can enhance the retrieval and integration of memories.

Imagine you have the fabric that holds the difficult memory stored in the very deep drawer. LSD is a substance that can act as a special key to unlock the drawer and allow you to feel and see things that were not felt or visible before.

It's as if a magical light shines on the drawer, making reaching inside and touching the fabric easier. You can start to pull it out bit by bit. As you do, you might begin to remember things you had forgotten or didn't fully understand.

3. **Ketamine.**

Ketamine is a controlled substance in the United States, so it's heavily regulated. It is not approved by the U.S. Food and Drug Administration (FDA) for treating mental health disorders, but it can be legally administered, off-label, by licensed medical professionals for this purpose.

Ketamine is known to have dissociative effects, meaning it can create a sense of detachment from one's body and surroundings.

It is believed that the substance's effects on the brain's neurotransmitters may facilitate the formation of new brain pathways and connections.

With ketamine, you see the fabric inside the drawer through a different lens. The dissociative effects of ketamine can create a state of altered consciousness that allows you to explore and examine your traumatic memories from a completely different vantage point.

NOT a Magic Pill

As I have mentioned before, these alternative treatments are not for everyone. You are responsible for your healing and your choices.

You might be called to include psychedelics in your exploration of self. Or you might not be interested or feel ready. Perhaps, you have medical conditions that prevent you from participating in these types of treatments.

Psychedelics are not a magic pill you take and --poof!-- all of a sudden, life is rainbows and butterflies. The opposite often happens. If I compare it to any pill, it would be the red pill Neo takes in The Matrix.

If you recall the red pill awakened Neo from the illusion he lived under. Psychedelics are just a tool. You can use this tool when you are ready to expand your understanding, and to confront the sometimes-harsh reality of the matrix of your life, in an accelerated way.

After Neo took the pill, he had to engage in many battles. His journey involved facing numerous challenges, including encounters with powerful adversaries. All to unravel the deeper mysteries of the Matrix. During this time, he learned to tap into his true potential.

Your healing is often a similar journey. It takes work, and taking the red pill is not a decision you should make lightly.

If you are interested in alternative treatments, it is essential that you educate yourself and seek medical advice.

Exercise caution and ask for recommendations from trusted individuals who have experienced treatments at the centers you are considering.

Don't rely blindly on my opinion or visit any of the places I mention in this book without conducting thorough research.

In the upcoming chapter, I will provide general recommendations and an overview of what you can anticipate when engaging in alternative medicine treatments. This information will assist you in approaching these therapies with greater understanding and preparedness.

I will also cover a few additional options for those not interested in the psychedelic route.

Hidden Memories

CHAPTER 29
Conscious Voyages

"An investment in knowledge pays the best interest."

– Benjamin Franklin

Psychedelic treatments are not to be taken lightly. Psychedelics have potential risks and adverse effects, especially when used irresponsibly or without proper guidance. They should always be used in controlled settings and under the supervision of trained professionals to maximize their therapeutic benefits and minimize potential risks. Additionally, individual responses to substances can vary, so caution and informed decision-making are crucial when considering any treatment.

When using state-altering substances for therapeutic purposes, finding a balance and exercising good judgment is of utmost importance.

Achieving balance means using the substance in moderation and being mindful of its effects on physical and mental well-being. Exercising good judgment involves making informed decisions about when and how to use them.

When it comes to psychedelic-assisted therapy or psychedelic experiences in general, it is crucial to consider something called set and setting. These terms refer to your mindset and to the physical or environmental factors surrounding the treatment or ceremony. Why you take psychedelics, where you take them and who is facilitating the treatment will largely define your experience.

Set

It is what goes on in your mind before, during, and after an experience. Your mindset, intentions, beliefs, and emotional state. It involves psychological readiness, expectations, and openness to the process.

- **Psychological readiness:** Refers to the reason why you want to undergo treatment. People who work with the medicines casually, out of curiosity, or because someone else wants them to "heal" don't have the best or most profound experiences.

  These treatments have the potential to be life-changing, and they often are. They are generally not easy or pleasant. Ayahuasca is a particularly powerful plant medicine. You will derive the most profound benefits if you are ready and willing to face your own life and to change it, if needed.

- **Expectations and openness:** It is essential to have an open mind and being receptive to whatever experiences may arise.

  Psychedelic treatments are highly individual and unpredictable and don't always conform to your preconceived notions or desires. Remember, the medicine gives you what you need, not what you want.

  If you go into the treatment with rigid expectations and those expectations aren't met, you might feel disappointed or even dismiss the experience as a waste of time. This mindset prevents you from recognizing the subtle blessings or teachings that might have occurred during the journey.

Setting

It is the physical and social environment in which the psychedelic experience occurs. It encompasses the physical location, ambiance, facilitators, helpers, or guides. I cannot emphasize enough how important this is.

Clinical Settings and Ceremonial Settings

- **Clinical settings:** Treatments take place in a medical or therapeutic space. Trained medical professionals, therapists, or facilitators lead the sessions. They have specific expertise in psychedelic therapy and often follow evidence-based practices.

  The primary goal usually revolves around therapeutic healing and personal growth. Sessions are structured with specific treatment objectives tailored to your needs.

- **Ceremonial settings:** Ceremonial settings are rooted in traditional or indigenous practices, often associated with plant medicines. Ceremonial settings are sacred environments, and the energy of the space helps create an atmosphere of reverence and respect. These ceremonies incorporate traditions, songs, and practices passed down through generations.

  The emphasis is still on healing and personal growth. Still, there is also an element of spiritual exploration and connection to nature. Ceremonies are usually led by shamans or experienced medicine people. A shaman is a traditional healer found in various indigenous cultures around the world.

It is said that a shaman is a "wounded healer." They often become proficient in their abilities by healing their own suffering or trauma.

Ideal Settings

- **Location and ambiance:** A thoughtfully chosen private location that ideally has access to nature can facilitate the journey.

  Lighting is very important since psychedelic experiences can be highly sensory and visually intense. Rooms are often dimly lit or dark to minimize visual distractions. Or you might be asked to wear a blindfold which helps you focus on your internal experiences rather than on the external world.

  Music is often played during treatments. The music helps you dive deeper into your journey. The different sounds, rhythms, and melodies can take your emotions and imagination on a roller coaster ride that facilitates healing.

- **Facilitators, medical professionals, or guides:** These people play a vital role in ensuring your safety during treatments. Despite precautions, unforeseen challenges can arise. Responsible facilitators prioritize safety and minimize risks, which leads to a more positive and beneficial experience.

The person or people facilitating the treatment should be knowledgeable about the substance they facilitate and have experience working with psychedelics.

An experienced facilitator who has done personal work using the substances they facilitate often has better insights and is better equipped to help others during treatment. I love how this is explained in Dr. Dan Engle's book, *A Dose of Hope*:

"You can't effectively hold space for others unless you understand what the journey is like. The more work you've done, the better you can help others in their journey. It is difficult to help others with things you have not addressed yourself."

Possible Dangers

- **Energetic dangers: (especially during plant medicine ceremonies):** During a psychedelic experience, your energy field becomes more open and sensitive. You might absorb imbalanced or negative energies if the environment is not cleansed and protected. This can, among other things, interfere with your energy flow, causing confusion or emotional turbulence.

- **Physical Safety:** Inadequate screening for medical contraindications or interactions with other medications can lead to adverse reactions. Taking psychedelics without proper preparation or without dosage control can lead to physical complications.

- **Ethical Concerns:** Psychedelics can alter your perception and boundaries, making you more vulnerable during the experience. An unsafe environment without knowledgeable guides can put you in physical and spiritual danger. Not everyone who offers treatments or ceremonies has your best interest at heart.

- **Lack of follow-up:** Psychedelic experiences are profound and transformative, often bringing up deep emotions, insights, and shifts in perspective. Without proper support, you may struggle to effectively integrate these experiences into your daily life. Talking to a therapist or counselor, who, besides listening to you, helps you feel and process your emotions, can be very beneficial.

Alternative or Complementary Modalities

Several approaches can be combined with psychedelics or used as alternatives to support healing and personal growth. These approaches go beyond the traditional "talking cure" by involving the body in an effort to release emotions that might be trapped. These approaches recognize the connection between physical sensations, emotions, and psychological well-being. See if any of these appeal to you:

1. **Somatic Experiencing (SE):** You can explore Somatic Experiencing, a technique Peter Levine developed that zeroes in on your body's physical sensations. This approach aids in releasing any trapped traumatic energy that might be lingering within your

nervous system. Its goal is to address and resolve the fight-flight-freeze responses associated with trauma.

2. **Eye Movement Desensitization and Reprocessing (EMDR):** Consider delving into EMDR, a psychotherapy approach utilizing bilateral stimulation through eye movements, taps, or sounds. By engaging in this modality, you assist yourself in processing and freeing up traumatic memories and the connected emotions. EMDR is thought to leverage your brain's natural healing capabilities.

3. **Trauma Release Exercises (TRE):** You might want to explore TRE, involving straightforward exercises that initiate involuntary tremors in your body. This natural shaking helps release accumulated stress and tension from past traumatic experiences. Dr. David Berceli developed this approach.

4. **Dance and Movement Therapy:** Experience the transformative power of dance and movement. Engaging in these practices offers you a channel to express emotions that might be challenging to voice verbally. Through movement, you can access and let go of these emotions.

5. **Acupressure and Emotional Freedom Techniques (EFT):** Try combining acupressure with Emotional Freedom Techniques (EFT). By tapping on specific points and focusing on emotions, EFT uses both physical touch and mental strategies to release emotional tension and restore balance. It's a simple way to help you feel better emotionally.

6. **Yoga and Tai Chi:** Engage in the ancient practices of yoga and Tai Chi, which meld physical postures, mindful breathing, and self-awareness. These practices can be instrumental in unwinding both physical and emotional tension within you.

7. **Mindfulness-Based Stress Reduction (MBSR):** Dive into MBSR, a practice that cultivates mindful awareness of bodily sensations and breath. This mindfulness approach helps you connect with and ultimately release any trapped emotions stored within your body.

8. **Breathwork:** Explore breathwork techniques like Holotropic Breathwork, which entails controlled breathing patterns to induce altered states of consciousness. This method may facilitate emotional release and provide valuable insights.

9. **Energy Work:** Delve into energy-based healing modalities such as Reiki, Pranic healing, and Qigong. These practices engage with your body's subtle energy

systems, tapping into the interplay between your physical and emotional states. By manipulating energy flows, addressing chakra imbalances, and connecting with a universal life force, these modalities offer holistic avenues for releasing trapped emotions and promoting your overall well-being.

Branches of a Tree

Regardless if you are interested in healing trauma using psychedelics or if you want to engage in body-based modalities, one thing is certain, healing extends far beyond your personal experiences.

The last chapter of this Part Three explores the intricate connection between trauma and generational imprints.

Much like the branches of a tree extend beyond its trunk, the legacy of trauma and healing also reaches beyond individual experiences. By acknowledging this, you gain insight into your own struggles and those of others, fostering empathy, healing, and the potential to break the cycle of inherited trauma.

CHAPTER 30
Old Burdens

"What we do now, echoes in eternity."

– Marcus Aurelius

Trauma is passed down across generations and can be imprinted in a community or family's collective consciousness or energetic field.

Many tribes and communities worldwide believe that the hardships experienced by parents resonate through the ages, impacting not only their children but also their children's children for up to seven generations.

Similarly, biblical verses, like Exodus 34:7, hint at the far-reaching consequences of ancestral experiences. The verse suggests that the "sins" or "errors" carried by previous generations are passed down upon the third and fourth generations.

The transferring or passing down of specific traits, behaviors, or patterns from one generation to another within a family is called transgenerational transmission.

You inherited physical traits like eye color or height from your ancestors. When it comes to trauma, imagine it as an invisible thread that winds through generations, impacting you much like those inherited physical characteristics.

And just as the scars of trauma can be passed down through generations, so too can the seeds of healing.

The Trauma Tree

Imagine a tree with deep roots and many branches. Each branch represents different generations in my family, and the roots symbolize the shared experiences and history that connect them.

Many generations of my ancestors are at the base of my tree. Some or many of them experienced the traumatic event of childhood abuse. This trauma became a part of their identity and influenced their thoughts, emotions, and behaviors.

The tree grew many branches, all growing from the same tree trunk. On my branch, I have my great-grandparents, my grandparents, and my parents.

The twigs on that branch are intertwined with painful memories and unresolved trauma from the previous generations. Some parents might have internalized the abuse they endured; others might have repeated the cycle with their children.

Now, we reach my generation, represented by me and my siblings. The branches of the tree continue to grow, carrying the weight of the trauma that has been passed down. But this time, there is a difference.

New twigs sprout from the branch, representing healing, resilience, and change. These new twigs grow and strengthen, positively influencing my entire family tree, shaping a new narrative, and breaking the cycle of childhood abuse.

In Your Grandmother's Belly

These generational cycles first came into my awareness when I read the book *It Didn't Start with You* by Mark Wolynn, a renowned therapist, author, and expert in inherited family trauma.

The book explains how traumatic experiences and unresolved issues from previous generations can be passed down through the family lineage.

These generational issues can affect your behavior and your emotional and physical well-being. He also mentions that trauma can affect how genes work and explains these genetic changes can be transmitted across generations.

The book talks about a notion that blew me away. A female fetus carries a lifetime supply of eggs within her ovaries before she is born. Your mother carried her lifetime supply of eggs when she was a fetus in your grandmother's belly. You come from one of those eggs, so a part of you has been inside your grandmother's belly.

You carry your own traumatic experiences and have also inherited the legacy of trauma that belonged to your mother and potentially even your grandmother. The genetics that shape you were molded by the relationships they navigated, the culture they breathed, and the world they knew.

Holocaust Trauma

In the book *Trauma and Memory: Brain and Body in a Search for the Living Past*, Peter Levine sheds light on the veracity of generational transmission.

In his clinical work with the descendants of Holocaust survivors, he observed frequent anxiety and depression symptoms.

Many individuals he studied recounted vivid and distressing experiences that seemed real but couldn't have happened to them because they didn't live through the holocaust.

He discovered that the events his patients recounted had occurred to their parents, not them. Surprisingly, most parents and grandparents had not shared those memories with his patients.

Don't Jump to Conclusions

Since trauma can be passed through generations, in some cases, medicines like ayahuasca can bring up ancestral memories and experiences, including trauma that originated and belongs to past generations.

Given this, it is imperative that if a memory of trauma, especially sexual abuse, comes up during treatment, you use discernment and self-reflection. It is essential to evaluate the new memory carefully and ask questions.

Questions You Must Ask

- Does this memory align with any patterns or behaviors I have noticed in myself or my family?
- Are there any unexplained emotional reactions or triggers in my life that could be connected to this potential trauma?
- Does this memory provide insight into my recurring relationship dynamics or challenges?
- Have I ever experienced unexplained physical symptoms or chronic pain that might be linked to this trauma?
- Do I feel a sense of resonance or familiarity with this memory, or does it feel completely foreign to me?
- Have I ever had unexplained feelings of fear or anxiety related to specific situations that could be connected to this trauma?
- Does this memory provide context or understanding for any unresolved feelings of shame or guilt that I have experienced?
- Have I ever had unexplained nightmares or vivid dreams that might be connected to this trauma? Or has my mind carried subtle breadcrumbs of clues?

- How does this memory fit into the larger narrative of my life, and how does it influence my understanding of myself and my experiences?

Talk to the Right People

Remember that there is still a lack of awareness surrounding memory storage and childhood trauma. So, it is imperative that you seek support from facilitators or therapists who are experienced in trauma work and who understand the science behind traumatic memory storage.

The help of a knowledgeable facilitator is incredibly beneficial in navigating these sensitive experiences. They can help you process and integrate these memories while providing a safe space for exploration and healing.

Echoes of Resilience

Healing is a gift that also spans generations; the echoes of your resilience reverberate through time. Just as the pain of trauma can be handed down, so too can the power of healing.

As explained by Shams Tabrizi, a 13th-century Persian poet, the notion that one person's healing can reverberate

through generations, both backward and forward, is a concept rooted in the understanding that our thoughts, actions, and emotions have a ripple effect on those around us and can shape the collective consciousness.

Addressing your wounds transforms your life and lays the foundation for a legacy of strength and renewal. What if your healing journey today becomes the catalyst for brighter tomorrows, not just for you but for those who will follow in your footsteps?

The seeds of healing sown today can blossom into a garden of well-being that nurtures not only your own soul but the hearts of generations yet to come.

PART 4
Emerging Phoenix

*"The only person you are destined to become
is the person you decide to be."*

– Ralph Waldo Emerson

Part Four of this book is about the months that followed
my initial visit to Costa Rica.

Shining light into the dark corners of my mind set me
off on an exploration and I couldn't stop half way. I needed
to follow my path until the end. I kept on remembering that,
as the American poet Robert Frost wrote, the shortest way is
always through.

My quest for knowledge took me to seek additional
treatments in South and Central America. I knew my effort
to heal my wounds would be worth it. Still, I had to pull
courage out from very deep within me to keep participating in
treatments, one after the other, knowing that they would likely
shatter my soul a little more each time.

As painful as the truth was, recovering my hidden
memories was the catalyst for my transformation. It pushed
me to unravel the tangled threads of my past and to recover
the pieces of my shattered self.

In these next pages, you will gain a deeper understanding
about the transformative nature of healing and the profound
beauty that can emerge from the depths of our hearts, even in
the face of life's darkest storms.

Stepping Out of the Train

This final section also centers around a vital aspect known as "integration." Integration is the transformative process of assimilating the insights and wisdom gained from psychedelic experiences into your daily life.

Imagine the psychedelic experience as boarding a train that takes you on an exciting, often long, and transformative journey. During the ride, you go through blizzards and beautiful landscapes. You encounter new ideas and have profound insights. But once the train ride is over, the real work begins.

Integration invites you to step into the metaphorical train station, check into a hotel, and take time to unpack your emotional baggage. This time allows you to organize your newfound insights and reflections so that they can take root in your heart and mind.

Integration empowered me to make lasting changes and improvements in my life. You will read about the steps I took to embrace my newfound insights and healing and how this integration allowed me to embark on a soul-enriching exploration within myself. It was not a straightforward path and growing was, at times, incredibly difficult.

This part is not just about my journey; it is an invitation for you to glean insights and wisdom that may resonate with your own experiences and challenges.

Take a moment to pause and reflect on the storms you've encountered in your own life. Think about how those experiences have influenced and shaped you as a person. Were you able to find transformative healing amidst the struggles? Explore the depth of your resilience and inner strength, and recognize the growth that may have blossomed from those tough times.

The emerging phoenix is a symbol of rebirth and resilience. Like the mythical bird rising from the ashes, you can become stronger and more beautiful when you continue to work on yourself.

CHAPTER 31
A Death Wish

"Someone I loved once gave me a box full of darkness.
It took me years to understand that this too, was a gift."

– Mary Oliver

There is much talk in our society about suicide. When we lose people to suicide, we always talk about them. However, there is less talk about the person who earnestly tries to kill her or himself and fails.

In a trapped person's mind, suicide seems like freedom, the only way out. Sometimes dying seems like the only way to escape painful circumstances. Surviving seems to rip that hope away.

If you or someone you know is struggling with thoughts of self-harm or suicide, seeking help is a sign of strength, courage, and self-compassion. Reach out to a trusted friend, family member, mental health professional, or a helpline.

Memory Snippets

As an adult, I could only access a few short memories from my childhood. Three of those memory snippets were from one day when I was eight.

On that day, I rode my bike around the empty pool of my house. It was a very large pool, and the deep end was about 12 feet deep or almost four meters.

The first memory snippet was of the moment I stood up, all bloody, at the bottom of the pool.

The second one was of my dad refusing to take me to the hospital if he had to ride in the same car as my mom.

The third one was of me at the hospital getting x-rays done and asking to see my sister Karina, who was on vacation.

We all viewed that incident as an accident. I came up with an elaborate story to explain the fall to my family.

Two details never made sense, though. The bike I was riding did not follow me into the pool; it stayed on top of the pool, far away from the edge. And my hands and arms were intact; in fact, my hands were not even scratched.

The Angles Held Her

During my treatment in Costa Rica, I asked the medicine to be shown what had happened during my childhood.

After the room went white and silent, the incident at the pool was the first complete memory that appeared on my "mental screen."

While watching the memory play out on the screen, I remembered that a thought came over me as I rode around the pool that day. I have had similar thoughts my entire life but always ignored them as an adult. That day at the pool, I didn't ignore it. The thought was simple yet powerful: "What if I don't stop?"

That day, I rode full speed toward the pool's edge and jumped off my bike. I dove head first and landed on the ground of the deep end; my hands had no scratch marks because I didn't try to stop the fall.

The doctors took countless images; they didn't understand how I had survived. I didn't break a single bone! "The angels held her," the doctors explained to my family. And I truly believe they did.

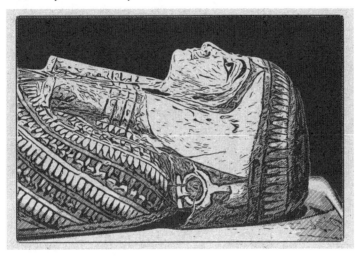

A Mummy

After the doctors checked me, they decided to keep me under observation for a couple of days. I remembered laying on the hospital bed; my left shoulder was throbbing. The top layer of the skin on the left side of my face was completely gone.

My entire head was wrapped in bandages, much like an Egyptian mummy. I was crying quietly and had one repeated thought: "No one is going to believe me. No one is going to believe me." I was desperate inside. But outside, I remained calm because my mom was sleeping on the chair beside me.

Ninety percent of incest victims don't tell anyone what is happening to them. Susan Forward makes this point in her book, *Toxic Parents*. She writes: "Sexually abused children realize early that their credibility is nothing compared to their aggressors'. It doesn't matter if the parent is alcoholic, chronically unemployed, or prone to violence; in our society, an adult is almost always more believable than a child. If the parent has attained a certain measure of success in life, the credibility gap becomes a chasm."

I felt entrapped in the cycle of abuse; my mouth and throat were tightly wrapped in layers of suffocating bandages, much like the literal ones that covered my face that day at the hospital. The fear of speaking out acted like ancient wrappings, sealing away the truth, keeping it locked in the depths of my being.

Just like a mummy preserved in time, pain and trauma stays hidden beneath the surface, unable to break free.

Who Do You Know?

The likelihood that you know someone who has survived abuse, including incest or other forms of trauma, is significant.

Suppose someone you know might be silently carrying the weight of past trauma behind their brave smiles and well-constructed facades. How can you be a source of support and understanding for them?

What actions can you take to create a safe and empathetic space where they feel comfortable sharing their experiences, should they choose to do so?

Embrace the power you have to make a difference in someone's life. Your compassionate presence may be the beacon of hope they need to navigate their healing path.

Why?

After processing the memory of my suicide attempt, I sat on my mattress in Costa Rica in shock. I asked myself "Why?". "Why did I try to kill myself?". When that question left my lips, my "mental screen" flickered to life again, revealing more long-buried childhood memories.

In those haunting flashbacks, I saw fragments of my past where I had endured unspeakable pain and suffered from sexual abuse inflicted by my father. The abuse started when I was three years old and lasted until before he died.

As the puzzle pieces fell into place, I realized that my darkest moments, which drove me to consider ending my life, were interconnected with the traumatic experiences I had buried deep within. The simple question, "why?" sent me on a harrowing journey through the depths of my soul.

A Safe Haven

When I left Costa Rica, I couldn't understand how, despite the abuse I endured, I had developed into a high-functioning child and adult.

I then read a passage from the book *The Body Keeps the Score* that helped me make sense of it. Dr. Bessel Van der Kolk recalls his experiences at the Children's Clinic at the Massachusetts Mental Health Center.

He writes that the center was filled with disturbed and disturbing kids. "They were wild creatures who could not sit still and who hit and bit other children, and sometimes even the staff. They would run up to you and cling to you one moment and run away, terrified, the next. Some masturbated compulsively; others lashed out at objects, pets, and themselves."

He then adds that the subjects in his study also lived in poverty in a depressed area of Boston, where they regularly witnessed shocking violence.

He explains, "research has firmly established that having a safe haven promotes self-reliance and instills a sense of sympathy and helpfulness to others in distress." He goes on to say about children who have a safe haven: "They get 'in sync' with their environment and with the people around them and develop the self-awareness, empathy, impulse control, and self-motivation that make it possible to become contributing members of the larger social culture. These qualities were painfully missing in the kids at our Children's Clinic."

Was I Loved?

In my twenties, I asked my mom and sister Karina about my childhood a few times. I asked, "Was I loved as a kid?" My mother looked stunned when I asked.

"You received so much love," she said. "I loved you so much, your siblings, father, aunt, cousins, and your siblings' friends. They all loved you very much. You were like the little mascot of the house."

I asked my sister the same thing and she said, "Melissa, you were my baby; I loved you like you were my daughter. I used to take you everywhere with me. Everyone in my university knew you. When you were four and five years old, you used to sit in the classroom and listen attentively to the teacher. You were friendly and a little shy. You loved me so much."

Even if I don't remember, I must have been loved. Because here I am, writing this book. Without the love I received from all other members of my family and their friends, I would not have survived my teens and adulthood years.

That love allowed me to remain functional. As Dr. Bessel Van der Kolk says, they provided me with a safe haven. It was not a perfect environment by any means. Still, it was much better than the environment most abused children grow up in, with zero love or stability.

Never underestimate the power of a loving home. Even an imperfect home like mine offered me some consistency. It was a buffer against the harshness of the rest of the world I lived in.

Can You Spot Hidden Clues?

Realizing that I grew up without overtly indicating what I was going through made me understand that not all abused children show obvious clues while being trapped in a cycle of abuse. Some kids might be getting lots of love from their parents, which creates a safe haven for them, while being abused by a grandparent or bullied by a classmate, for example.

Have you ever encountered children who seemed to be masking their pain beneath a veneer of smiles and laughter? Could there be a hidden world of trauma lurking beneath the surface, unbeknownst to those around them?

It's vital for you, as a caring adult, to be alert and attentive to the children around you, whether they are your own children, family members, friends, or children in your community.

Pay attention to any subtle shifts in their behavior, sudden personality changes, or signs of distress. Note any regression to earlier developmental stages or unexplained aggressiveness or withdrawal.

By remaining vigilant and compassionate, you may become the beacon of hope for a child who desperately needs it. Your empathy and understanding might be the catalyst that empowers them to break free from the chains of silence and seek help.

My Sudden Change

After my mom and sister told me how much love I received. They both said the same thing. That one day, I just changed; I stopped loving them back. They never understood what happened; they thought it was a normal stage of my development and personality.

My mom told me that she felt she had lost me. She said, "When I was away in New York, I lost you to your father." To her and everyone else, the relationship with my dad appeared healthy. So, she focused on my other siblings because she thought my father was taking good care of me.

I knew something had changed when I was a kid, but since I didn't have an explanation for it either, I came up with a very unscientific belief; in my twenties, I told them: "I think that when I hit my head, I forgot I loved you both. Because it was so strange, one day I just didn't love you anymore."

This numbing mechanism became a chronic pattern of self-protection. As a result, it became difficult to connect with my emotions, maintain close relationships, or be fully engaged in the present moments.

A Mother's Guilt

My mother didn't know what to look for; mental health awareness was not as prevalent back then. She has grappled with intense feelings of guilt since finding out about what happened during my childhood. She has embarked on her own healing journey. Self-forgiveness is not always easy, but she strives to find peace within her heart with determination and love.

Your Feelings and Your Voice

If you find yourself in a similar situation as my mother, you are not alone. Many parents, grapple with past decisions and actions. They often wish they could have protected their children.

If you have survived abuse and carry the heavy burden of silence, understand that deciding to keep silent in the face of trauma is a deeply complex and individual response. The weight of shame, fear, and self-blame can make it incredibly challenging to speak out.

Remember that the shame and silence you endured were not your fault. The power dynamics and fear that kept you silent were imposed upon you by the circumstances, and you coped in the best way you knew how at the time.

As you release the weight of the silence you carried, or the weight of not having realized what was happening to loved ones around, allow yourself to step into the light of empowerment and self-compassion. Your past does not define you. Celebrate your resilience, and know that you can create a future where your voice and the well-being of your loved ones are cherished and honored.

CHAPTER 32
The Funeral

"Our primary purpose is the help others. And if you can't help them, at least don't hurt them."

– Dalai Lama

When I was younger, I used to say to my mother, "You know, Mom, there are two things I could do if I wanted to. One is to kill myself, and the other is to kill someone." The certainty in my heart when I said that always made me feel strange.

Lying inside a cave deep in the mountains of Ecuador, I understood why I could utter those words with such conviction. I had tried to kill myself and failed. And as it turned out, I had succeeded in killing someone.

After Costa Rica, I researched different healing modalities and plant medicines. San Pedro medicine, in particular, captured my attention. I found a place that served that medicine in Ecuador. The retreat was appealing because it was deep in the mountains, and the medicine grew all around.

Two Little Frogs

In my high school graduation speech, I told a story. It was about two little frogs that fell into a bucket of milk. One gave up and died, but the other kept paddling until the milk turned into butter, and she was able to leap out to freedom.

When I arrived in Ecuador, I was just like the frog who kept paddling in the milk. Just as she couldn't predict her salvation, I couldn't foresee the full extent of my healing.

My time there was simultaneously devastating and magnificent. I held onto hope, knowing that with each effort, I was building the strength to overcome challenges that once felt insurmountable.

I stayed for several weeks at that retreat. It is called *Casa del Sol.* It is in Vilcabamba, a town located in a beautiful area known for being one of the places in the world where people live exceptionally long and healthy lives.

This retreat is very special; I was held with so much love by everyone there. I connected with the mountains, the water, and nature like never before.

During my time there, I met many incredible people who also traveled from distant parts of the world to drink San Pedro and other plant medicines.

The Funeral March

I got my first menstrual cycle while visiting a friend. I was 14 years old. My friend had gotten a beautiful bouquet of red roses from her dad when she got her period. I hoped my dad would buy me one too. He did not.

After serving the San Pedro, the medicine man and medicine woman often led the group into the mountains. We ended up resting in an open cave on one of the days.

One of the facilitators was playing an instrument I had never heard before. It looked like a mini piano but sounded like a mix between an organ and an accordion. It is called a harmonium. Everyone was enjoying the music, everyone but me.

Every time I heard the notes, they took me to a funeral march. I was at a funeral, mourning a death. Red roses laid on top of an urn. I cried bitterly for a long time. I was mourning the death of my innocence. I mourned the loss of my virginity to my father.

Weight Gain

My father used to drive across the city several nights a week to pick me up for dinner. When I was 15 years old, I went through a pizza phase. I wanted to eat pizza every night. He would buy me a large pizza, and I would devour it whole.

My mother told me years later that my father had spoken to my sister because I was gaining weight, and he was worried about my eating habits. That summer, he planned a trip to New York. He usually took several of us on trips at the same time. But on that trip, he only invited me.

My mom and friends commented on how pretty I looked when they saw me again a few weeks later. I had lost a lot of weight. In fact, all my clothes were new, because the ones I took on the trip were too loose on me.

In the mountains of Ecuador, with the help of the San Pedro medicine, I remembered what happened before and during my trip to New York.

The sexual abuse escalated after I became a woman. My weight gain was not only due to food. I was pregnant at 15. That summer, my dad flew with me to New York to get rid of that life, a boy, about four months old. As a reward, I received new clothes and shoes and was allowed to eat as much whipped cream as I wanted.

Me in New York with my father

Giving Birth

In the retreat, they also served other medicines. One night, I drank ayahuasca. That treatment involved intense bodily sensations. When I was deep in the medicine, I felt pregnant. At first, I wondered if, somehow, I was thinking of a future pregnancy. Soon I realized that the sensations of pregnancy felt familiar. It dawned on me that those feelings and sensations belonged to my past.

That night I understood the energetic connection that exists between a mother and her baby, especially when the baby is in her belly. This connection is often described in ways that go beyond physical and scientific explanations.

The intensity of the experience overwhelmed me. I felt like I was in labor. After a long process, I started to give birth, and the energy of the baby boy left my body.

This energy represented the emotions, thoughts, and memories associated with the abortion that I had suppressed. The healing I experienced during that night went beyond my personal healing though. I felt the full weight of the generational burdens I carried.

Black Purge

Connecting to a generational collective intelligence involves tapping into the wisdom, experiences, and knowledge of past generations to gain insights and guidance in the present.

This reservoir of information spans across time. You might be able to connect with this reservoir through deep reflection, meditation, or altered states of consciousness.

I tapped into my ancestors' reservoir during that same treatment in Ecuador. Toward the end of the night, I entered a blinding darkness. I pulled black strings out of my body. I purged intensely, and my vomit was as black as charcoal.

As I purged, I understood that childhood abuse ran on both sides of my lineage. My father's lineage was especially dark. Many children from his lineage also suffered the abuse I had suffered. The strings I pulled were the strings of trauma endured by my ancestors.

It was as if that unconscious dark thread that perpetuated the repetition of that cycle of trauma had been cut.

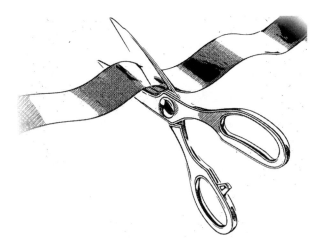

Making Amends

I have never wanted children. I felt repelled by children all my life. I would look at mothers and their babies and I would feel pity for the mother; I felt their child was a punishment. That night in Ecuador was significant because my opinion of children started to shift right after that treatment. I no longer despised them; I felt compassion and love for them.

As I began to understand how my early life experiences had shaped me, I decided to talk with Miles, my ex-husband's son. By that time, he was a teen. The idea of this amazing boy carrying a scar because of my inability to love him was too much for me to bear.

Even though we both lived in South Carolina, less than 20 minutes away from each other, I had only seen him once in three years. After I came back from Ecuador, I invited him to go for a walk on a local beach.

I told him about my childhood. I explained that I had been unable to love him, not because he was not lovable, but because I didn't know how to love him.

I apologized for all the times I ran away when he arrived. I was not really running away from him; I was running away from my childhood fears. My subconscious feared I would repeat the same harm to others, particularly children. This fear is not uncommon among survivors of childhood sexual abuse. It can lead to aversion or discomfort when being around children.

This young man listened to me and, at least at a rational level, understood it all. We hugged and parted. I thought that was all I could do.

A Second Chance

A year later, I received a text from him: "Hey, it's been a while since I've reached out to you since we're living two completely different lives now, but I've been thinking about you almost every day since the last time I saw you. Just figured I'd check up on you and your life and see what's new. I figured we could do something together when you are back in town."

That text filled my heart with joy. I invited him to visit me a few weeks later, and he accepted. We had the most beautiful weekend. We talked non-stop and bonded in more ways than I can explain.

At the end of the weekend, he said in an emotional tone, "Melissa, I think you should reconsider not having children because you would be a wonderful mother." My eyes watered,

Recent photo of Miles and I

and I said, "Do you know what else I will be wonderful as? A grandmother."

I am grateful for Miles; I love him as a son. And if grandkids come, I will be honored to be a bonus grandmother.

Not a Death Sentence

Trauma only feels like a death sentence if it goes ignored or worse if it's unknown.

Alice Miller describes this eloquently in her book *The Drama of The Gifted Child*:

"The damage done to us during our childhood cannot be undone, since we cannot change anything in our past. We can, however, change ourselves. We can repair ourselves and gain our lost integrity by choosing to look more closely at the knowledge that is stored inside our bodies and bringing this knowledge closer to our awareness. This path, although certainly not easy, is the only route by which we can at last leave behind the cruel, invisible prison of our childhood."

Through my profound encounter with Miles, I understood that we have the power to transform ourselves from unconscious victims of our past into accountable individuals in the present.

Many people unknowingly let the past dictate their actions, avoiding any exploration of their history and persisting in the shadows of their repressed childhood experiences. Fear and avoidance linger, perpetuating outdated dangers that no longer exist. Unseen memories and suppressed emotions silently dictate their every move, stifling growth and potential.

Are You a Hostage?

Take a moment to reflect on whether your past is holding you hostage. Are you unconsciously letting past experiences dictate your present actions and decisions? Can hidden memories or suppressed emotions be guiding your path, preventing you from embracing growth and fulfillment?

It's never too late to change the course of your life and positively impact the lives of your loved ones. As you journey through my story, I hope you are filled with hope and inspiration that moves you to embrace change, transformation, and the pursuit of a better life for yourself and those you hold dear.

CHAPTER 33
The Explosion

"If you never heal from what hurt you, you'll bleed on people who didn't cut you."

– Tamara Kulish

Some traditions believe energy gets exchanged during sexual intercourse. And that in heterosexual encounters, the vagina is especially susceptible to the energy of the masculine. People in these traditions often use the sacred plant medicine tobacco as a powerful energy-clearing tool.

The mass production, marketing, and consumption of cigarettes have disconnected the act of smoking from its original ceremonial and spiritual context and have diminished the sense of reverence and respect for tobacco.

The tobacco used in ceremonies is not the same as the commercial tobacco products used for smoking. In ceremonial contexts, tobacco holds deep spiritual significance. It is considered a sacred plant by many indigenous cultures and spiritual traditions. It can heighten your focus, ground you and expand your perception.

One night while in Ecuador, I underwent another interesting treatment. I was joined by six women and a medicine woman. The treatment involved energetic or spiritual work related to the reproductive organs, including the uterus and vagina.

Uterus Cleansing

In Chapter 22, I wrote about samskaras, the energy patterns that get blocked within the heart. Indigenous cultures believe energy can also become stuck or blocked in various body parts.

The idea behind releasing energies from a woman's vagina and uterus is based on the belief that unresolved emotions, trauma, or stagnant energy can accumulate in these areas, potentially leading to physical, emotional, or energetic imbalances.

When intercourse happens in a harmonious, loving, and sacred setting, that energetic exchange can create a balance and synergy between the two partners, enhancing the overall experience of intimacy and connection.

An unhealthy, traumatic setting or where there is a lack of emotional connection can lead to an imbalance or disruption in the flow of energy within the body of the partners.

Hapé powder and applicators

Release of Sexual Energy

With that in mind, we were told to roll a little cotton ball between our fingers for each person we were ever intimate with.

We put the little cotton balls with healing plants and flowers inside a pot and filled it with boiling water. Traditional cooking pots in the Andean region are made of clay and are very sturdy.

All seven of us sat in a semi-circle. The medicine woman blew a finely ground powder called Hapé up our noses. Hapé, also known as Rapé, is typically made from powdered tobacco leaves (Nicotiana rustica) and other medicinal plants, such as tree barks, seeds, or ashes from sacred plants.

The effects of Hapé can be very intense. That night it helped us to connect with ourselves, our bodies, and higher states of consciousness.

We were told to squat on top of the pot so the vapors of the water could bathe our vulva. Then we were instructed to contract and release our vagina. The tightening and releasing of the muscles of the vagina is thought to create a pumping motion that helps release and distribute sexual energy throughout the body.

After a few minutes, something interesting happened. The sturdy clay pot that was in between my legs exploded. It didn't just crack; it literally exploded into small pieces, sending hot water everywhere.

Photo of the broken pot

Your Sexual Exploration

Energy flow is real, and that night a lot of pent-up sexual energy was released from my body.

No matter your beliefs about energetic exchanges during intercourse, it's crucial to recognize that sexual encounters can profoundly affect your psyche and body. These intimate moments can leave lasting imprints that influence your emotions and overall well-being.

To ensure positive and empowering experiences, practicing mindfulness is key. Being conscious of your intentions, setting clear boundaries, and communicating openly with your partner all contribute to creating a healthy and respectful encounter. This approach allows you to navigate intimacy with greater clarity and emotional resilience.

CHAPTER 34
Metamorphosis

"The past is never dead. It's not even past."

– Willian Faulkner

During metamorphosis, a caterpillar undergoes an astounding change. Before it emerges as a butterfly, it becomes goo inside the chrysalis. Its tissues and cells literally break down into a liquid.

Amid that total chaos, a group of specialized cells remains intact. These cells contain the blueprint for the butterfly's body parts, such as wings, legs, eyes, and antennae.

Through my plant medicine treatments in Ecuador, I built a metaphorical chrysalis and became goo. Inside my chrysalis, I dissolved the first 16 years of my life. I disintegrated my beliefs and dissected my emotions.

During my last night there, my figurative cells turned that goo into a butterfly, and I became ready to take flight and embrace a new chapter of my life.

In My Chrysalis

That last night in Ecuador was dark and cold. Sometime after drinking the cups of ayahuasca, I sat on my shins, with my chest on my thighs. The backs of my hands were pressed against the floor, and my face rested in them.

I had been in that position for a long time before I understood what I was feeling. I had blankets around me and on me. I was a caterpillar in a chrysalis.

Until that night, my treatments in Costa Rica and Ecuador had revolved around my childhood. But on that final night, the treatment was about my life in the present.

I was in so much pain in my chrysalis. My present life was filled with heartbreak and confusion. During this Ayahuasca treatment, my thoughts revolved around David, the man from my Tony Robbins year.

Though I hadn't seen him in a long time, he had stirred up my soul in such a way, that my life was never the same after meeting him.

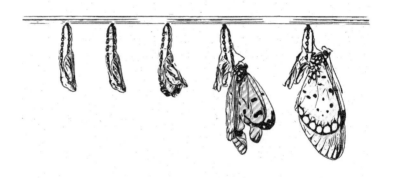

From Goo to Butterfly

I was afraid of leaving my chrysalis. At one point, a beautiful song called "El Abismo" by Alonso Del Rio came on. In that moment of confusion and metamorphosis, one of its verses, translated here, touched me deeply:

"And even if you don't understand

In every death there is a birth

That's why it hurts to be so alive."

When I heard that part, I raised up and opened my arms wide as if they were my butterfly wings.

That night, I just opened my wings and became ready for flight. I was not able to soar high above the mountains and revel in the beauty of the landscape of my present life yet.

The following day, I went down to the tattoo parlor and tattooed the words "In every death there is a birth" over my heart.

During my treatment I understood that I had to say goodbye to the pieces of me that craved love and attention from those who could not give it. I felt I had to say goodbye to David. Or that, at least, a part of our journey needed to die.

I didn't know how to let the idea of him go, but I decided to try. Still, I held on to the hope that, as the tattoo on my chest read, in that death there was also a birth. I hoped our paths would eventually cross and that we would find ourselves walking in the same direction when they did.

The Spiral of Healing

Even though I was in deep pain and confusion, I knew I had turned a page that night. I didn't revisit my childhood experiences in any treatment for a year.

In Colombian traditions, particularly within indigenous cultures, the path of the medicine is associated with the path of patience. This concept emphasizes the importance of patience and endurance in the healing journey and the pursuit of spiritual growth.

Healing is a big word. When I first embarked on this journey, I expected the path of healing to be a straight line pointing up. I was disheartened and disappointed in myself during the year that followed my time in Ecuador when I stumbled again over hurdles that I thought I had already "healed."

At the end of that year, I came across a profound revelation: the path of healing and growth resembles a spiral. It unfolds as an ever-evolving, rising spiral without a definitive endpoint, comprising cycles of revisiting and reworking past wounds, traumas, and challenges.

The idea is that when you circle back to a familiar wound, trauma, or behavior pattern, you gain a deeper understanding. You look at things from a different or higher perspective. You expand and transform a little more each time. You respond to the challenge differently.

My post-Ecuador time was nothing short of magical. It was full of opportunities for learning and growth. Ultimately, it guided me to a place of deep understanding and empowerment, reminding me that healing is an ongoing process that unfolds with each turn of the spiral.

Your Spiral

Consider how this spiral path manifests in your own life. Have you encountered familiar wounds, traumas, or behavior patterns that resurface? Instead of feeling disheartened, recognize that each revisit offers an opportunity for deeper understanding and growth.

Picture yourself spiraling upward, gaining new perspectives with every turn. The spiral path is a sacred dance of transformation, where challenges become stepping stones, guiding you towards profound shifts in perception and response.

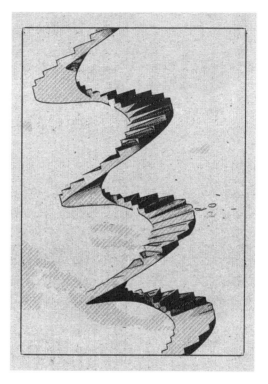

CHAPTER 35

From Shadows to Light

"Your visions will become clear only when
you can look into your own heart. Who looks
outside, dreams; who looks inside, awakes."

– Carl Jung

I grew up feeling like I was a bad person. I felt my heart was black, rotten. During one of my initial ayahuasca treatments in Costa Rica, I mentally reached into my chest and pulled my heart out.

I held it in my hand and looked at it in disbelief. It was beautiful. It was pink, fluttering, beating, and doing what hearts do. It emanated a yellow light; it glowed.

The sight of my beautiful heart terrified me. I put it back in my chest and went into a panic attack. Perhaps my heart was once a diamond in the rough, and all the healing pressure I was under just made it more brilliant.

The Shadows

It took me weeks to integrate that experience and to accept that, just like a diamond, my heart reflected light. From that moment on, I started to work on my "shadows."

Shadow work draws from the theories of Carl Jung, a renowned Swiss psychologist. Jung suggested that the shadow is an integral part of your psyche and contains both negative and positive aspects.

By consciously acknowledging and embracing these aspects of yourself with compassion and acceptance, you experience a deeper sense of wholeness and spiritual expansion.

Your dark shadow involves the unconscious thoughts, emotions, desires, and behaviors that you deem unacceptable or incompatible with your self-image.

The dark shadow represents the hidden or repressed parts of your being, including your fears, insecurities, unresolved traumas, and socially conditioned patterns.

There is another shadow that is easily overlooked. It is sometimes called the "golden shadow." It refers to the positive qualities, talents, and potentials you have disowned or denied within yourself.

These are the aspects of your personality that you perceive as positive, admirable, or desirable, but which you haven't embraced or integrated into your self-image for various reasons, such as societal expectations, self-doubt, or fear of standing out.

The golden shadow can include traits such as creativity, intelligence, compassion, strength, confidence, or other beautiful qualities.

All shadow work can be challenging and uncomfortable. However, great healing happens when you acknowledge and embrace your shadows, since they are both part of who you are.

Your Shadow

When you understand your perceived weaknesses and strengths, you become more self-aware. You grow emotionally and develop resilience. Embracing your authentic self gives you back your power so you can live in alignment with your values.

Reflect on the following:

*   **Unconscious Influences on Decision-Making.**
    Can you recall times when your unconscious thoughts or fears influenced significant decisions in your life? How might acknowledging these hidden influences change the way you approach decision-making in the future?

*   **Embracing Your Positive Qualities.**
    Think about the positive qualities or talents you admire in others. Do you possess any of those traits? If so, do you have a tendency to hide them? How might embracing and showcasing these qualities enhance your life and the lives of those around you?

- **Exploring Relationship and Career Patterns.**
  Consider any recurring challenges or patterns in
  your relationships or career. How might these be
  connected to aspects of your dark shadow that
  need acknowledgment and healing? How could
  understanding and integrating your golden shadow
  contribute to breaking these patterns?

- **Accepting Your Authentic Self.**
  Reflect on your self-image and the parts of yourself
  you tend to downplay or ignore. What beliefs or fears
  have prevented you from fully accepting these aspects
  of who you are? How might embracing your authentic
  self lead you to a more fulfilling and purposeful life?

- **Envisioning a Transformed Future.**
  Imagine a future where you have fully embraced
  both your dark and golden shadows. How would
  your relationships, career, and overall happiness be
  transformed? What steps can you take today to embark
  on this empowering journey of self-discovery and
  growth?

Like Attracts Like

When you accept yourself unconditionally, you become
more compassionate. You can also understand others better;
as a result, your relationships expand and deepen.

The law of attraction is based on the belief that like
attracts like. It suggests that the thoughts, emotions, and
energy you emit into the universe will return similar energies
or experiences to you.

The energy you emit, whether positive or negative, influences the types of people you attract into your life. Exuding positive energy makes you more likely to draw in individuals with similar positive vibes. Conversely, if you project negative energy, you may become surrounded by people who resonate with that energy.

Even though I experienced heights of pain I never thought possible during my months of discovery, I felt at peace like never before. I was grateful for the opportunity to rebuild myself, and I started to exude positive energy. I began to attract and, more importantly, to keep close, amazing people in my life.

The Rainbow Colors of My Soul

I met Gerald and his wife, Maya Rose, during my Tony Robbins Platinum Year. They were a gorgeous couple; Gerald had a blue Mohawk back then. They talked about spiritual things and about the magical retreats they organized, which are called Legendary Retreats. I thought they were crazy hippies and wasn't able to fully take in what they were all about.

I was in a different place when I ran into Maya and Gerald again, not by coincidence, during my second week at Rythmia. At that time, I was ready to welcome them into my life.

Lisa Nichols is a motivational speaker, author, and personal development coach known for her inspiring and empowering messages. In one of her YouTube videos she talks about how sometimes people see us through beautiful lenses, and at first, we need to borrow them, so we can see our beauty too. Maya Rose and Gerald wore lenses that allowed them to see the rainbow colors of my soul before I knew there was a rainbow in there.

I attended my first Legendary Retreat a month after I finished my time in Ecuador. It provided me with beautiful opportunities to play, to be a child again. During this retreat in Mexico, I started to rewrite my childhood story into a happier one.

A Tribe of Friends

When my journey started, I couldn't have imagined how many wonderful people I would meet. I have been held, seen, honored, and loved like never before. My ever-expanding tribe of friends is full of people who cheer me on when I am on the right track and tell it to me straight when I am not.

Their companionship and empathy provided a safe space for me to explore, heal, and grow during the months following my time in Ecuador when I integrated and processed what came up during my treatments.

Queen Zeena

I am blessed to have many fantastic women in my circle of friends. I am proud to belong to a tribe of incredible women. Women who align their lives with their values, beliefs, and desires.

I am especially grateful to one woman. During one of my breathwork and meditation retreats, I experienced my second soul recognition. I opened my eyes after meditating and I saw a woman walk by.

I had seen her walking around during the week. But, at that moment, I really saw her. I saw her pain and sadness and felt compelled to say something.

I stood up and walked towards her chair without thinking about what I would say. "Hey Zeena, just so you know, we are going to be friends forever," I said. Then I smiled and walked away, leaving both of us very confused!

Meeting Zeena has been a blessing. She has been a friend and sister to me. She laughs a lot. Her laughter helps me realize how uptight I have been my entire life. She saw the crown on my head and pointed at it until I saw it too. She always makes sure I don't let it drop.

Recent photo of Zeena and I

Your Tribe

Reflect on the power of meaningful connections and the importance of building a tribe of supportive and empowering friends in your own life. Do you have a tribe of friends who genuinely support and encourage you on your journey? Do they create a safe space for you to explore, heal, and grow?

If you haven't yet found the connections or the tribe you desire, remember that like attracts like. Work on becoming the person you want to attract into your life. Cultivate the qualities, values, and authenticity that resonate with your soul.

Embrace the mindset that your dreams are within reach and that you are deserving of the connections and relationships that align with your heart's desires.

Stay patient and open-hearted as you continue your journey. Remember that every step you take towards becoming the best version of yourself is a step towards attracting the right people and opportunities into your life.

CHAPTER 36
A Tiny Seed

"A palm tree is not afraid of a storm;
it is just another dance."

– Matshona Dhliwayo

Looking at the palm trees above my tent, I realized I had become one of them on my journey. I had started as a rigid tree, and slowly and painfully, I had become a supple palm tree.

The first Legendary Retreat I attended was in Tulum. While I was there and during the following months, I had to bend in the strangest of angles, just like a palm tree, in search of the bright sunlight.

After a very bumpy taxi ride, I arrived at a beautiful house that sits with the Caribbean on one side and wetlands and lagoons on the other.

Thirty of us sat for dinner around a long table the first night and shared our names. Just six days later, some of these people became part of my soul family. Human connection is ever present; bubbling on the surface, eager to be given a chance to expand.

2/22/22

In spirituality and numerology, dates with repeating numbers or sequences are often considered significant. February 22, 2022, is one such date, as it contains the repetition of the number two.

Some view repeated numbers as a sign of alignment with the universe or as divine guidance. This particular number sequence is a reminder to seek balance and harmony in life, to trust one's intuition, and to focus on nurturing relationships and connections with others.

On the evening of 2/22/22, we all gathered around a beautiful bonfire under the starry sky. We sat on hand-woven mats and pillows and got ready for a long breathwork and meditation session.

Before the breathwork session in Tulum

A Closed Heart

During that session, my intention was to open my heart and release my fear of receiving and giving love. I wanted that so badly.

During the breathwork I felt so much love, but my heart still felt closed. Well, it was closed for everyone but David. A man I had not seen in years and whom I had never even kissed. I probably sound like a broken record, bear with me just a little longer.

My feelings and views of what our interactions meant had started to change after my time in Ecuador, yet, I was still hoping that one day he would just walk back into my life.

David and I had spoken a few times during the previous years, so I knew that he was divorced, was going through his own journey, and that it was not an easy one.

I was angry about not hearing from him more often. Yet, mostly I was sad, confused, and frustrated as to why I couldn't let him go.

Losing Love

When the breathwork ended, I sat by the fire and started talking to a friend.

He asked me, "What is your intention tonight?"

"I want to open my heart and release my fear of receiving and giving love," I said.

"How was your breathwork?" I asked him.

"I just realized I need to leave my girlfriend," he said.

"Why?" I countered.

We continued talking, and at some point, he told me about a woman he loved, with whom he felt a magnetic soul pull. He explained that he had never felt anything like it before and has not felt it again.

"I am waiting to feel a connection like that with someone again, and I don't feel it with my current girlfriend," he said.

I told him how meeting David had set my soul on fire. I said I felt we had magnetic magic between us, much like him and that girl did. I told him the story of my treatment during my last night in Ecuador, and that I felt I had to let that connection go.

My friend said, "Call him right now!"

I laughed and said, "You are crazy! I am not calling him"

"Invite him to come; we will make space for him," he said.

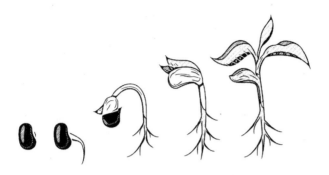

Fast Growing Sprouts

Have you ever planted a seed and watched it grow? Seeds are usually fairly small; some are even tiny. Despite their small size, they include all the information necessary to grow into majestic trees or wonderful flowers.

A tiny seed was planted in my mind that evening. I realized the following morning that the seed had sprouted overnight. I grabbed my phone, typed a message, and sent it to David:

"Hi, can you call me at 9:30 a.m. your time? I have something to ask you."

I planned to invite him and give him reasons why he should come. I was three hours ahead, so the phone call would happen at 12:30 p.m. my time. At 12:30 p.m. I grabbed my phone and sat in a quiet corner.

Everyone was getting ready to go to the beach to jump in the ocean. I watched them go just as I watched the minutes pass. 12:30, 12:31, 12:40, 12:48, 12:52.

Plants need three things to grow: light, water, and nutrients. That tiny seed in my head had started to germinate with the light of hope, the water of love, and the nutrients of possibilities. At 12:52 p.m. the hope, love, and possibilities disappeared, and the tiny sprouts began to die.

We All Got Naked

I stood up and walked to the beach, leaving my phone behind. As I took each step, I felt the sand under my feet. My jaw dropped when I arrived at the beach. Everyone was naked, and they were putting mud and masks on their bodies.

Without thinking, I took my bikini off and joined them. Most of us had never been in such a situation before. We were laughing and absorbing that new and unknown sense of freedom. It was not sexual. No triggers or red flags were going off in my mind. It was all simple, liberating, and beautiful.

We danced under the sun as the mud dried. When the clothes came off, we were just humans. No male or female, just people. There was no judgment or competition. We were just kids playing freely.

I felt at ease and said to myself in a loud but sweet voice, "My heart is opening." The heart has to break to open, they say. Mine broke a little more, and in turn, it started to open.

I Wanna Feel What Love Is

I realized the sprouts of hope, love, and possibilities were still alive in my mind. I wrapped them in a wet paper towel, just in case. I knew one day they would grow. It just didn't seem that David wanted to be the one witnessing them grow into beautiful sunflowers.

I put on my ear buds and started to play a beautiful song called, *I Want to Know What Love is*, by Foreigner. I sat by the shore, looked into the blue sky and sang the lyrics out loud as a prayer:

"I wanna know what love is

I want you to show me

I wanna feel what love is

I know you can show me"

I had prayed many times before. This was the first time in my life that I felt I was talking directly to the universe. To God. The next night, my prayer was answered.

CHAPTER 37
Synchronicities

"Unless it's mad, passionate, extraordinary love, it's a waste of your time. There are too many mediocre things in life. Love shouldn't be one of them."

– Rebecca Lynn Jenkins

A Jack-in-the-box is a kid's toy. It's a box with a crank. Music plays as you turn the crank, and pressure builds up inside the box until Jack jumps out.

During my Platinum Year, I tried to push David into boxes he didn't want to be in as tightly as you push Jack into the box before you close the lid.

I turned the crank a few times during the months that we shared until the lid popped open; he jumped out and left me startled. The more I chased him, the more he avoided me and ran.

I was thinking about this Jack-in-the-box analogy the day I danced naked on the beach. My friend, the one who instigated my text to David, walked toward me, wearing only his birthday suit. He asked me if I had heard back.

"No," I said.

"Maybe send him something else," he suggested.

"I am done," I replied.

He then told me about the many ways the Oxford Dictionary states humans relate to each other. Mother, sister, cousin, friend, lover, husband, son, partner, to name a few. He told me that certain people in his life didn't fit in any of those boxes.

As he walked away, I thought: "He has a nice butt." Then I analyzed the piece of knowledge he had just dropped on me.

I remembered how special the beginning of my friendship with David was and the immense pressure I put him under during most of our interactions later in the year. I needed him to fit into one of my preferred boxes. I was terrified of losing that connection. I needed someone to love me. I needed a savior.

No Box to Fit In

That morning I understood many things more clearly, so, I typed another text:

"A friend told me that there are like 27 ways for humans to relate to each other defined by the Oxford Dictionary. I haven't been able to fit you into one of those boxes. You don't fit in the friend's box, we haven't explored the lover's box, and we are not in the acquaintance's box, for example.

You said that I knew you and saw you. And I felt I did. You are special to me as a human; you lit my soul on fire with your presence in the past. And at that time, I just wanted us to fit into one box. I tried to force us into it, as you know.

I want you to know that I don't think we fit into any of those typical boxes. I'm extending the invitation to meet somewhere and catch up. No agenda, no box to fit in. I will be in Tulum for a few days after my friends leave this Sunday morning. Can you come?

I want to know why our worlds collided years ago. I can't explain why, but deep down I feel we should meet. Maybe your rational side thinks that it makes no sense to meet me, yet if a part of you still wants to meet, I hope you will come."

Carl Jung coined the term synchronicities, which is widely used today. We experience synchronicity when a meaningful coincidence or event occurs in a way that seems to go beyond mere chance. Synchronicities are viewed as significant moments of connection between the inner and outer world, carrying deeper symbolic or spiritual meaning.

David sent a text back and told me that he had booked a trip to Tulum months ago. He was actually arriving in two days with some friends.

A Magical Tool

Your breath is a magical tool that can help you explore different worlds inside yourself. Different breathwork techniques can activate the body's relaxation response and stimulate the release of endorphins and other neurotransmitters, which can induce a sense of expanded consciousness.

During the final night of the retreat, we had another intense breathwork session. The effects of breathwork can be very powerful. Alternate or altered states of consciousness, very similar to those reached with psychedelics, can be reached with just breathwork.

Losing Consciousness

As I lay under the stars that night, my prayer: "I want to know what love is," was answered. I lost consciousness for a couple of minutes. When I came back to myself, I could barely speak. A stream of tears had run from my eyes, down my cheeks, and into my ears. My ears were filled with tears.

They were tears of joy; I felt an overwhelming amount of love. It was as if a whole four-year university curriculum on love was downloaded into me. I was shown what love was, and for the first time, I felt it.

It was one of the most spiritual instants of my life. A lot changed in that moment. Thirty-seven years of religious fears were gone. Only love for God, the universal magic, and all people remained.

At that moment, I realized that I didn't just try to fit David into boxes; I had been trying to mold myself into what I thought others wanted me to be my whole life. But something clicked inside me, and I felt I didn't need to fit into those boxes anymore.

In that instant, without realizing it, I also let go of many limitations, inhibitions, and judgments I had been holding onto. I unlocked my body's dance language, a secret dance of authenticity and liberation.

CHAPTER 38
With or Without You

"Dance, when you're broken open. Dance, if you've torn the bandage off. Dance in the middle of the fighting. Dance in your blood. Dance when you're perfectly free."

– Rumi

For much of my life, I had a terrible fear of dancing. I developed a belief during my early childhood and reinforced it through the years that told me I couldn't dance and had no rhythm. So, I never danced.

The night I finally met David again, I discovered that dancing is medicine. And I have been enjoying its healing powers ever since.

Up on Stage

In the early 2000s, after I'd moved to England, I flew back to Florida to see another U2 concert. I had lost a lot of weight, and the gray English weather had turned my skin pale.

I took a center spot on the rail, right in front of the main stage. When the show started, all my worries disappeared. I was high on music again. I sang every word while jumping up and down. I even jumped up and down during the slow songs. I still do!

"With or Without You" started to play. Bono walked toward the front of the stage and pointed at me. Yeah, me. In no time, two security people grabbed me, one on each side.

They pulled me over the railing as if I was weightless and planted me on the stage.

I have a big mouth, physically big. That night, it expanded in all directions. I was in total disbelief.

Bono hugged me, and I hugged him back; we held each other for the duration of the song. It was such a magical moment for me. It made me so happy. I carried that feeling with me back to England.

Bono and me in Tampa, FL

Mysterious Ways

About a year later, U2 announced a tour in Australia. I was walking around London one day and fell in love with a pair of jeans. They only had one pair, but I had enjoyed England's famous curries too much, and the pants were two sizes too small.

I said to myself, "I'm going to wear these jeans the night Bono picks me up on stage again." After he'd pulled me on stage in Tampa, I was very hard on myself because, in my shock, I felt I didn't do anything; I just smiled. I vowed that if I ever had that privilege again, I would not let it slip; I would do something unique.

I purchased tickets for five shows, three in Sydney and two in Melbourne. All my U2 friends know that, during those years, being on the front row meant lining up days in advance. We would all sleep outside the stadium and eat scraps just to jump like crazy for two of the best hours of our lives.

The jeans fit just in time for the fourth show. They were tight, but I got in them. That night, Bono pointed at me again, and up I went. This time the song they were playing was "Mysterious Ways."

Once on the stage, I just whispered in his ear, "Bono don't make me dance, please." I think he saw the fear in my eyes. So instead, he jumped into my arms, and I carried him like a baby.

I hold that memory close to my heart. After that, he pulled me up again in different cities and during a couple of tours. Each time, I managed to dance a little more. But it was so hard. I was so self-conscious, and my body felt as rigid as an oak tree. Still, I can say Bono was my first dance partner, which is pretty cool!

Me carrying Bono on stage in Australia

Our Spiral

Fast forward again to the last night of the retreat in Tulum. Up until that point, moving my body with ease was challenging. It was as if the accumulated trauma had not only locked my mind, it had also locked my body.

The breathwork that night put me in an altered state of consciousness. And somehow, during the minutes when I lost consciousness, I released the blockages and restrictions that had bound my body and mind, especially regarding movement and dancing. However, it wasn't until a couple of nights later that I truly grasped the profound transformation that had taken place within me.

Both David and I found ourselves attending the same music festival in Tulum with our respective groups of friends. Remarkably, our tables were very close.

The spiral of growth kicked in during that festival. I had been looking forward to seeing David again for a long time. By then I had done a lot of healing, yet meeting him showed me how much I still had left to grow.

Two things happened. First, I was flabbergasted by how handsome he looked. That did not help me at keeping a level head.

Second, all the familiar feelings instantly bubbled up to the surface, the beautiful ones and the not so beautiful ones. The fears, the pain, and the sadness.

Twist of Fate

We both were equally uncomfortable. We spoke briefly. David said some beautiful things about our interactions. How meeting me had affected his life as deeply as meeting him had affected mine. I saw the pain in his eyes and felt the pain in my heart.

When he spoke to me, I could see the little boy inside of him, guarded and closed off.

I wanted to open my heart fully, hoping he'd meet me there, but he remained distant. It was as if "a sleight of hand, a twist of fate," had left us wrapped in a thicker blanket of uncertainty.

He said he couldn't give me what I wanted; in truth, neither of us knew what the other wanted. In the end, we both stood there, two souls entangled for a moment but ultimately going on separate journeys.

The Night the Music Danced Me

One magical thing happened that night: I danced. Out of nowhere, I tapped into the energy and rhythm of the music. My movements were fluid, effortless, natural, and uninhibited.

I entered a state where my body and movements became entangled with the music and the space around me. I became attuned to the vibrations of the dance floor. For the first time in my life, I was in what people call a state of flow.

In psychology, body language is often associated with emotions and inner states. I have observed repeatedly, with much curiosity, that there seems to be a correlation between the amount of personal growth a person goes through and their ability to take space on a dance floor and to dance with their arms above their head.

When people have gone through healing work or have reached a place of happiness and self-assurance, they feel more comfortable expressing themselves freely and openly, which is reflected in their dance movements. Imagine the dance floor as a stage where their journey takes center spotlight.

The dance floor is a reflection of their evolution, a platform for them to rewrite their narratives, and a mirror for you to ponder: What stories does your dance tell?

Dancing in Tulum

342

Rushing His Healing

Seeing David again was beautifully painful. I was glad we talked, but I had overestimated my emotional growth when it came to him. And once more, my overly hopeful expectations had set me up for disappointment. I was heartbroken.

I didn't feel I needed him to save me any longer, but some part of me still needed to save him. I wanted him to be happy so badly that I was still trying to rush his healing and growth.

If you try to rush or interfere with someone else's healing, you deny them the chance to learn and overcome obstacles on their own terms. In a way, you attempt to rob them of the opportunity to cultivate resilience, self-awareness, and the skills necessary so they can navigate future challenges.

It took me months to process our interaction. My heart needed to heal a little bit before I could see things from a different perspective. I finally understood that healing is a deeply personal journey. The challenges people experience are valuable lessons that contribute to their personal development.

My Role in My Suffering

I took a hard look at myself, and during the following months, I dove deeper into the role I played in my own suffering. The times I ignored my better judgment and made choices that led me to a depleted emotional state. The times when my fears drove my life and took control of my actions. The times I avoided facing my behaviors and refused to change them.

My heartbreak made me want to continue exploring even
more of myself. I had no idea what lay ahead or where I was
headed, but I trusted the process implicitly.

Your Role

Taking responsibility for your role in your suffering
doesn't mean blaming yourself entirely. By exploring and
acknowledging your part in the narrative of your life, you can
rewrite the script and find new paths to happiness, fulfillment,
and inner peace.

Consider the following:

- **Taking Responsibility for Change:** Are there
recurring challenges or patterns you wish to change in
your life? How might accepting responsibility for your
role in these situations lead to positive shifts?

- **Exploring Emotions and Reactions:** Consider a
recent difficulty or heartbreak you've experienced.
What emotions and reactions arose during that time?
How might exploring your responses shed light on your
role in the situation?

- **Challenging Limiting Beliefs and Fears:** Are there
any self-limiting beliefs or fears that might influence
your decisions and contribute to your suffering? What
steps can you take to question and challenge these
limiting beliefs?

- **Cultivating Self-Compassion:** How would you
describe your relationship with self-judgment?

Are there ways you can cultivate self-compassion and understanding as you navigate your journey of self-discovery?

- **Growth Through Ownership:** Can you recall a specific instance when taking ownership of your role in a challenging situation led to personal growth and healing? How did this newfound awareness influence your subsequent decisions and actions?

CHAPTER 39
Lock and Key

"People come into your life for a reason, a season, or a lifetime."

– Brian A. Chalker

Pretty Woman is one of my favorite movies; I have watched it many times since I was a teen.

The final scene portrays Edward and Vivian standing on the fire ladder. He fears heights but climbs the fire ladder all the same. They meet halfway on the steps, and he asks, "So what happened after he climbed up the tower and rescued her?" "She rescues him right back," she replies. They kiss passionately, and a happily-ever-after is implied.

When I was younger, I secretly wished I was Vivian, minus the prostitute part. As women, sometimes, we grow up hypnotized by the idea that we need saving. We are taught that we are half of an orange, and we spend our existence looking for our other half.

Special Classmates

I don't believe people meet by coincidence. We attract significant connections into our lives. If this is the school of life, we have classmates with whom we learn more than with others.

David and I are that special kind of classmates. We have served as a mirror for each other. Our connection has forced us to look at unresolved issues, traumas, and emotional

346

wounds. In a way, we have been each other's sources of inspiration for personal growth and transformation.

We have been ever-present in each other's spiral of healing. Every interaction has always been full of learning opportunities. Meeting him all those years ago propelled me into the journey I have described throughout this book. I am forever grateful for that.

Catching a Big Fish

Dr. Dan Engle writes in *A Dose of Hope*, "The medicine does not give you a fish. It doesn't even teach you how to fish. It just points out where there are fish."

It's up to you to go fishing deep in your soul. Sometimes you catch little sardines; other times, you catch a big fish.

About eight months after Tulum, I did a psilocybin treatment, and I happened to catch a much bigger fish than I expected.

As I mentioned earlier in the book, unprocessed emotions are at the root of trauma. During my psilocybin treatment, I processed many emotions I had "bypassed" regarding David.

I always tried to avoid feeling my emotions when it came to him. I usually invalidated them by creating reasons in my mind as to why he was or was not acting in a certain way. I would push aside feelings of sadness, loss, uncertainty, unworthiness, regret, disappointment, or pain without delving into the root causes.

During my treatment, I understood that, for me to heal, I didn't have to decide if his actions were right or wrong. What was important was to process the emotions his actions elicited in me and the effect those feelings had on my mind and body.

During the psilocybin treatment, I felt the emotions associated with each experience I had with him that had left a wound. Those wounds had already scarred over, but I had to open them again to clean up the infection that was festering under the surface. I had a lot of "suffering debt" to pay after ignoring my feelings for so long. It was a very hard treatment.

Changing the Lock

As I emerged from that treatment, I sent David a text. The last part of the text said, "I put the key to my feelings in your pocket a long time ago, hoping you would find it one day. And I have been hiding my heart under a rock ever since, waiting.

I realized I need to change the lock because the key I gave you doesn't fit anymore, and if you happened to find it, you probably threw it as far away from you as you could, for reasons only you know."

Dissolving My Soul

I didn't expect him to reply, yet when he didn't, I entered a new stage of development.

Spiritual alchemy is a metaphorical and transformative process that draws upon the principles of traditional alchemy and applies them to inner growth and spiritual development.

Similar to how alchemists sought to transmute base metals into gold, spiritual alchemy seeks to transmute the "base" aspects of the self, such as negative thought patterns, limiting beliefs, and emotional baggage, into higher states of consciousness and wisdom.

The days after that treatment were very dark. I went into another "dark night of the soul." I felt an incredible amount of inner turmoil and suffering.

I experienced a spiritual crisis and a fleeting loss of faith, that left me profoundly empty and questioning my life's purpose. I felt physically sick; lots of energy was purged from my body. I dissolved different parts of my soul. Although it took some time, just like an alchemist, I started to transform the base metals of my emotions into the precious gold of self-love.

Your Wounds and Scars

When considering your life, ask yourself: Are there unresolved emotions from past experiences lingering beneath the surface? How have those emotions affected your mind and body over time? Have you developed scars over those wounds, hoping they would heal on their own?

Just as the psilocybin treatment helped me cleanse the infection beneath the surface, you can also free yourself from the weight of unresolved emotions. I encourage you to find spaces and practices that help you explore your feelings. It may be through therapy, mindfulness, or simply taking time for self-reflection.

Embrace the opportunity to heal and release the "suffering debt" that has accumulated.

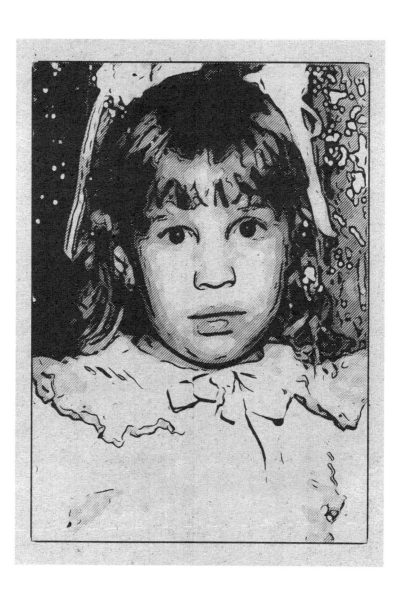

CHAPTER 40

Stolen Childhood

"So much of the healing of our world begins in healing the inner child who rarely, if ever, got to come out and play."

– Vince Gowmon

What do people mean when they talk about "your inner child?" Regardless of age, you carry inside of you a part that is still like a child. It's a special part that holds your innocence, curiosity, and sense of wonder about the world.

Your inner child is full of creativity and imagination. It's the part of you that dreams big, believes in magic, and sees the world in a unique and beautiful way. It's a part that loves to laugh, play, and express emotions freely.

On the next part of my journey, I met my inner girl. My encounter with her guided me through the maze of sensations and emotions that had haunted me most of my life.

Four months after my Psilocybin treatment, I flew to Costa Rica and returned to Rythmia.

During the final treatment day, I briefly chatted with Dr. Jeff McNairy, the Chief Medical Director at Rythmia, who has over two decades of experience in healthcare. I shared my concerns about a missing piece in my healing journey, explaining how I still struggled to fully move forward.

We decided to set up an appointment, and we met later that afternoon. Sitting in his office, he asked me:

"Have you talked to your inner child, Melissa?"

"No, I haven't, actually," I answered.

"Perhaps that can be a good intention for tonight's treatment," he added.

She Didn't Use Words

That night's treatment was the last treatment of the week. It began at seven p.m. and continued until the next morning. I was at ease as I entered the room that night. I didn't know what to expect, but I knew what my intention would be.

I went up to the medicine man and whispered my intention into the cup: "I would like to meet the girl I was once, my inner child."

I repeated the same drill with my second cup and finally my third. I didn't feel much after the first two. After the third, I lay back down and drifted off to sleep.

Shortly after, I woke up completely frightened. My arms were tightly wrapped around me. I was unable to speak; I was panting. I knew what was happening immediately.

"Hi," I said. "You are safe."

At that moment, I was talking to myself. Not me, the woman laying on that mattress; I was talking to me when I was four years old. I was finally meeting my inner child, and she was terrified.

She didn't use words. She was too little to explain her feelings with words. She gave me a glimpse into her life through her emotions. That deep, paralyzing fear was the fear she felt, and during those minutes, I felt it too.

A Little Girl's Fear

I had been to so many lessons at Rythmia that their recommendations were ingrained in my mind. There were a series of questions that I always asked when faced with uncomfortable emotions during treatment, and I asked them to myself that night:

1. "What am I feeling?" I asked. I answered, "fear"

2. "Do I feel this emotion often in my life?" I asked. "Yes," I answered.

3. "When was the first time I felt this emotion?" I asked. After years of not knowing, my inner child was showing me the answer to the third question: I was four years old the first time I felt that kind of fear.

The fear I didn't deal with when I was a child grew into the fear that had been with me for so long. It was just concealed beneath a strong woman's façade.

Cancer of the Mind

I remained laying on my mattress, overpowered by fear, and a voice came into my mind and said with certainty:

"If it feels good, it can't be bad."

It was a familiar voice. It was my father's voice, and those were his words. That is one of the sentences he used to create doubt in my innocent mind. So, he could cross my physical and mental boundaries. When I understood that, I felt betrayed. My father's betrayal felt like a stab to the heart.

With that sentence, he blurred the line between appropriate and inappropriate behavior. It is such a powerful line of reasoning for a four-year-old psyche to process.

Every part of me realized how an adult can so easily take control of a child's mind. I sat up on my mattress, and yet again, my mouth opened wide and stayed like that until I processed the shock. I wept and released an immense amount of pain.

Before that night, I knew abused children and adults often kept traumatizing circumstances a secret. But in that instant, the innocence and fear of my inner child helped me understand the depths of mental manipulation children endure. Incest is a form of cancer. I see it as a cancer of the mind.

A Split Mind

I rested for a bit, and then my inner girl came back. I knew she was back because I found myself hugging my knees to my chest. I was screaming, but no sound was coming out of my mouth.

My mind split, and I saw myself lying calmly on a bed in a catatonic state. I was about 12 years old, and she showed me her internal hysteria.

I was feeling all the emotions that were going on inside of her. My heart was racing, and my mind felt like a pressure cooker on the verge of exploding. Yet my body was paralyzed.

I was completely taken over by two emotions. I felt an overwhelming amount of shame and guilt.

I had felt that powerful combination only once before, during my first Ayahuasca treatment 14 months earlier. If you recall, I asked the medicine to "show me who I had become." During that treatment, I was transported to my father's funeral, and a wave of shame and guilt engulfed my heart. Back then, I couldn't comprehend why the medicine led me there or why I was experiencing those overwhelming emotions.

As it turned out, my intention had been fulfilled that first night. At 12 years old, as my father stimulated me sexually, I had become a girl full of shame and guilt. And that is who I had been for most of my life.

In her book *Toxic Parents*, Susan Forward explains this prevalent "side effect" of abuse. She writes: "Just as verbally and physically abused children internalize blame, so do incest victims. However, in incest, the blame is compounded by the shame. The belief that 'it's all my fault' is never more intense than with the incest victim."

The consequences of my interactions with my father are not unique to me; they are distressingly common among abuse victims. One, in particular, is especially devastating. My 12-year-old self showed me that one too.

Lighten Your Load

Take a moment to consider how you see yourself now as an adult. Any unproductive emotions you feel could be rooted in roles that didn't belong to you as a child, but you took them on due to the circumstances you faced.

Are there emotions or beliefs you hold as an adult that you haven't fully understood or explored? Do you sometimes display behaviors or reactions that seem puzzling or unfamiliar? What might be the origins of those emotions and patterns?

If you find yourself experiencing certain emotions or behaviors without fully understanding their origins, I encourage you to embark on your exploration with resilience, courage, and persistence. Embrace this journey as an opportunity to delve into the depths of your psyche and unravel the mysteries that shape your present reality.

As you explore the effects lingering in your life, be gentle with yourself. Embrace the emotions that arise and grant yourself the grace to heal. Remember that you are not alone on this journey; seek support from loved ones, therapists, guides, or support groups if needed.

CHAPTER 41
A Magical Sunrise

*"Look at how a single candle can both
defy and define the darkness"*

– Anne Frank

Imagine the world as a magnificent garden full of flowers.
Each flower represents someone who has endured a unique
form of childhood trauma. Just as some flowers yearn for
sunlight, water, and nurturing to flourish, people require love,
safety, and support to truly thrive. Sadly, numerous childhood
environments lack these vital ingredients, causing the symbolic
blossoms of the children's hearts to wither and fade.

Children who face traumas often carry a deeply rooted
belief into their adult lives: they see themselves as damaged
or broken. This conscious or hidden perception acts like an
invisible mark on their forehead, shaping how they perceive
themselves and their role in the world.

Giving Pleasure

Throughout my life, a fire has burned within me, a fierce
passion and zest for life. Though at times it remained hidden,
it never truly faded away. However, I couldn't escape the
feeling that something was missing when it came to intimacy.
I wanted that fire to burn during moments of sexual play,
but I struggled to fully receive pleasure. That struggle left me
yearning for a deeper connection and fulfillment.

To cope, I immersed myself in the art of giving pleasure to my partner. While I genuinely enjoyed this aspect, it also provided a shield, allowing me to avoid being on the receiving end as frequently. The act of giving became a way to navigate the void in me.

Shutting Down

One of the most common consequences among those who survive sexual abuse is blocking or diminishing physical pleasure.

My marriage highlighted all my emotional triggers. Even though I had no conscious recollection of the abuse I suffered, my body and mind remembered that I had been used by the man I loved and trusted the most as a child.

A year into my marriage, amidst a profound lack of love and respect, I felt sex was all I was good for. So, my body shut down.

I rationalized this in several ways:

"There is no love in the marriage."

"I am not attracted to him."

"The religious conditioning about sex being a sin is still strong."

And yes, all of those arguments were true, but the deeper explanation was shown to me by my 12-year-old self during that same treatment in Costa Rica.

As a teenager, I experienced the often uncontrollable physical responses to sexual stimulation. The way I was touched by my father felt good.

The thoughts of that 12-year-old were:

"I shouldn't feel good."

"He only continues doing this because I feel good."

I took the blame for his actions and trained my body during the following years to block pleasure. As a result, when I felt unloved in my marriage, my body responded much like it did when I was a kid. It numbed down my pleasure.

A sense of detachment from my body had haunted me my entire life. I felt free as soon as I grasped its origin. Knowledge gave me back my power. However, as we've explored before, awareness alone often falls short. I continue to actively reshape my perspective on intimacy and dismantle the lingering old patterns that persist. Growth takes time, and patience is paramount.

Do You Need to Connect?

If you feel disconnected from your emotions, ask yourself: Do I know why this disconnection exists? Are there behaviors or attitudes that arise during intimate moments that I struggle to explain? Do I carry wounds or beliefs that prevent me from fully embracing joy and vulnerability?

There may be moments in your life when your body's responses act like mirrors of past experiences, numbing down pleasure or creating barriers to intimacy. By exploring those patterns with curiosity and self-compassion, you can unlock the door to reclaiming your power over your emotions and experiences. Psychedelics are especially effective in aiding such explorations.

End of the Dark Age

The guides at Rythmia explain that the first intention, "Show me who I have become", is the one that usually takes longer to attain. After you feel you know who you have become, they encourage you to move to a second and third intention.

The second intention is: "Merge me back with my soul, at all cost" And the third one is: "Heal my heart." The guides say that the third intention comes almost instantly once you get the second.

Even though that last night in Costa Rica was painfully dark, when the morning came, I experienced one of the most beautiful moments of my life. Those last two intentions were fulfilled.

During the night, the door to a hidden part of my mind opened, and I met a child, an innocent girl. Without words, she took me to the most horrific moments of her life. I not only watched those moments, but I also felt them in my own skin and bones. She showed me her fear, pain, sense of absolute betrayal, shame, and guilt.

That girl was me, and that night I allowed myself to feel those emotions just for a few hours. My adult mind processed them and understood their effects on me.

I felt like a ton of bricks dropped off my shoulders. The bricks carried the illusion of a father. They were heavy and hard to keep up. I watched them break apart as they hit the ground. Even though I was in shock, I was liberated.

Hours later, I opened my eyes and realized the room I was in was not so dark anymore. I felt incredibly grateful for the light that illuminated the space around me.

That light signaled more than the start of a new day. It was the end of the 38-year dark age that had obscured my life.

Turning onto my belly, I propped myself up on my elbows and I let my chin rest on my hands. I gazed at the sun's rays, and the sky blushed with shades of pink. The birds welcomed the new day with their cheerful chirping. At that moment, I fell in love with that sunrise and with life.

A Blooming Flower

Throughout my entire healing journey, I painstakingly gathered the fragments of my shattered soul. That night I put them all together again, and immediately my heart was healed.

Something magical happened during those 12 hours. I fell in love with every aspect of who I was. From the vulnerable child within me to the turbulent teenager and the woman I had become, I found pride and love in each phase of my journey.

Like a flower blooming after a drought when it finally receives water, I felt the dormant parts of me stirring back to life.

With each realization, a new petal unfurled, exposing a strength that had been resting beneath the surface. The scars of my trauma became a testament to my resilience. I watered my soul with self-compassion and felt myself blossoming again.

Each step of my healing journey was like the gentle touch of a gardener, tending to the tender parts of my being. That morning, I knew that no matter what storms may come, I had found the power within myself to bloom again and again.

For the first time, I embraced myself with unwavering love. As I smiled, a promise formed in my heart: "No matter what the future holds, I will always cherish and love myself loyally."

Sitting at Rythmia after a ceremony

Healing Your Heart

What dormant strengths lie within you, waiting for the nourishing waters of self-compassion? What scars might one day become testaments to your ability to endure and flourish?

If you have been on a healing journey, what fragments of your soul have you gathered along the way? If you haven't gotten started yet, imagine the fragments of your soul, like pieces of a mosaic, coming together in the future to heal your heart. Are you willing to do the work?

Recognize that emerging from your own darkness often demands unyielding determination and relentless effort. If any aspects of your life are still in the shadows, view it as an invitation to seek the light with steadfast dedication.

CHAPTER 42
My Imperfect Heart

*"Your task is not to seek for love, but merely
to seek and find all the barriers within
yourself that you have built against it."*

− Rumi

Keeping your promises to yourself is at the root of
self-love; it includes recognizing and honoring your limits.
Whenever you keep one of those promises, you re-train your
mind and body. You tell your inner child that you can be
trusted and teach him or her that they are safe.

Throughout my journey, I realized that even though I was
compassionate and kind in most areas of my growth, I was not
compassionate or kind when it came to my sexuality.

I compared myself constantly to other women. And I
am not just talking about comparing myself to women who
experience multiple orgasms, vaginal orgasm, and squirting
orgasms. I am talking about the fear of not being enough
sexually and the assumption that some other woman is.

I got some insights into that fear during a psilocybin
treatment I did three months after I left Costa Rica.

A Painful First Half

About an hour after taking the mushrooms, I started to
cry bitterly. At that moment, the full weight of a realization hit
me. I felt that I had never had sex with someone I loved.

Actually, it was worse. I realized that I have never truly made love to anyone in my entire life. I processed that pain and grieved for a while.

I told Cheryl Fraser the story over dinner a few weeks later. Cheryl is a friend and the author of *Buddha's Bedroom*. She listened to what I said and replied: "Melissa, I don't want to bring darkness into this, but you have had sex with someone you loved."

I stared at her for a few seconds before the aha moment came. I knew I loved my father as a child and loved him after his death. I just never considered that I also loved him during the moments of abuse.

In the limited world of a child, there are few options for love and comfort. Unfortunately, in incest situations, the abusive parent is often the main source of such care. This creates a complex and challenging dynamic where the child's need for love and security becomes entangled with the harmful behavior they endure.

This new realization helped me understand better the second part of that psilocybin treatment.

A Beautiful Second Half

During that same treatment, I started conversing with a made-up masculine energy. He was telling me how much he wanted to make love to me. I turned into my teenage self. I was in disbelief. With amazement in my voice, I asked him:

"Really? Do you think you would like that?"

"Yes," his tone was eager.

"And you would like to make love to me just how I am? For who I am?" I asked.

"Yes," he said lovingly.

I realized then that although I had been learning to love myself, I still had trouble believing a man would love me. Me as I am, me for who I am.

That he would love my imperfect heart and soul instead of just loving the idea of a woman who is there to provide pleasure.

My heart filled up with an immense amount of gratitude in that moment. I felt so appreciated, loved, and desired.

Harmful Behavior Patterns

It's healing for women and men to explore their sexuality and to embody their bodies. However, it's crucial to recognize that not all paths of exploration lead to healing. Some can be re-traumatizing or devaluing.

In an effort to fix something within yourself, you might inadvertently put yourself in situations you don't want to be in. This behavior is not limited to abuse victims; it's a common coping tool many adults use to silence their pain and disconnect.

Peter Levine sheds light on this sad truth in his book, *In An Unspoken Voice*, he writes: "When their loneliness becomes too stark, traumatically disconnected individuals may seek increasingly more unrealistic (and sometimes dangerous) hook-ups... Having had a neglectful or abusive childhood predisposes them to chaotic relationships.

These individuals continue to look for love 'in all the wrong places'-a folly the song reminds us of."

During my treatment, I had another profound realization: tying my sense of worth to what I could offer rather than who I truly was had led me into harmful behavior patterns.

For example, I noticed I had engaged in sexual experiences because I felt I needed to fix something inside me. I also felt a sense of obligation toward my partner, even when he didn't value our time together, which left me questioning my self-worth.

Furthermore, I linked my self-worth to how well I performed during sex, often going to great lengths to exceed my partner's expectations. If I sensed any shortcomings in fulfilling those desires, I often took it personally and felt broken.

During my treatment, I finally understood that I lost a little piece of my soul every time I was intimate with someone I didn't love or who didn't love me. I realized that during those occasions I betrayed the teenager in me who is so eager to re-paint the past with the colors of true intimacy. When my treatment ended, I promised her I wouldn't betray her anymore.

Honoring Yourself

Take a moment to contemplate the importance of exploring your sexuality and embracing your body, but also recognize the significance of doing so in a healthy and healing way. Ask yourself: Have I ever found myself in situations that seem to trigger past wounds or that dimmish my self-worth?

How are my past experiences influencing my choices in relationships and intimacy?

Consider the impact of seeking validation and worth through what you can offer rather than embracing your true self. Have you ever found yourself sacrificing your well-being or compromising your boundaries to please others?

As you delve into your own journey of self-discovery, remember that healing is a courageous and transformative process. Embrace the parts of yourself that may have felt disconnected, and seek to find true intimacy and connection in a way that honors your worth and authenticity.

CHAPTER 43
Unconditional Love

"Love is all about guts. If you have it, you fight with the world. If you don't, you fight with yourself."

– Heenashree Khandelwal

I was seated in my house not long after my psilocybin treatment, when it dawned on me that I had been waging a tremendous battle inside my head and heart.

I realized that I had been fighting very hard not to care for David since the moment I met him. First, because he was married. Later, because he appeared not to care about me and I felt terribly silly caring about him.

The Power of Acceptance

That battle was exhausting. I had conflicting thoughts, emotions, and desires that drained my energy and mental resources. At that moment, on my couch, something beautiful happened.

I was breathing through my nose, but I felt I was really breathing into my heart. My heart felt open. I finally accepted that I loved David. I had always loved him. And that was Okay.

There were no conditions attached to that love.

I didn't need to explain it to myself, him, or anyone anymore. My friends were tired of hearing about it. I was tired of it myself.

For the first time, I didn't need him to do anything. I didn't need him to call or to show up in my life. More importantly, I didn't need him to love me back. I just sent him love and muttered under my breath:

"David, I hope you become everything you are meant to be."

I smiled, and a sense of peace washed over me. The last words a dear medicine man told me a year prior were, "Melissa, you just have to accept." I didn't know what he meant then. But sitting in my home, on my couch, I understood.

If you recall, I mentioned earlier that there are five stages of grief: denial, anger, bargaining, depression, and acceptance. It took me 4 years to move through those five stages when it came to David.

Acceptance helps you face the reality of your situation, including any pain, challenges, or losses you may be experiencing. You have to accept first, then the healing process can start. In accepting, you release tremendous amounts of inner resistance.

The day I accepted my feelings and understood that what people do (or don't do) is the real them, I freed up my mental and emotional energy to focus on self-care and my happiness.

The Pursuit of Happiness

You might notice that in pursuing happiness, you often get caught up in the external world, seeking love and validation from relationships or achievements.

A big shift happened in my life when I stopped chasing happiness. I have heard many times that happiness is something you cultivate within yourself. I had always thought it was a cliché; it is not. Getting to that mindset and keeping it requires work, yet, the effort is worth it.

I visited Sayulita in Mexico a few months ago. It was warm, and the air conditioning stopped working during the night. I opened the windows and got attacked by mosquitoes. When I woke up, I was sweaty, tired, and itchy. I looked up from bed and saw the ocean out my window. I remembered words my friend Dan told me:

"You have to make a conscious effort to tune into the frequency of happiness every day."

Happiness doesn't come naturally or consistently for most of us. So, I quieted my mind the best I could. Then I listened to one of my favorite songs, danced a little to get my energy up, and went on a MacGyver-style exploration to find the beach I had spotted from my room. I worked out on the shore, went swimming next to pelicans, and felt happy. I had tuned into the frequency.

It is easier to tune into the frequency of happiness when on vacation in Mexico. I started practicing happiness when it was easier or when I was having a good day. Eventually, gratitude became second nature. Now, with the mental muscle memory I've developed, I find moments of happiness even during challenging days.

When I shifted my focus from seeking happiness externally to cultivating it internally, I tapped into an endless reservoir of contentment.

In Sayulita after my swim

Reclaiming Love

Joseph Campbell wrote about the hero's journey that "The ultimate aim of the quest must be neither release nor ecstasy for oneself, but the wisdom and power to serve others."

While writing this book, I realized that I was at the final stage of this particular hero's journey. The one that started in Costa Rica all those months ago. It is said that in the final stage the hero returns home with lessons and treasures to share with others.

My journey has been so blessed. I have learned so many lessons. This book is the ultimate treasure I bring back and its true value lies in sharing it with you. These pages have been an open invitation for you to embark on your own transformative journey.

Another gift I bring back is a love story. We all want stories to have a happy ending. Look at us, over 25 years after Titanic was released, we are still debating if both Jack and Rose could have fit on the wood.

I have been searching for my epic love story my entire life. I feel at rest now, not because I have the king of my heart by my side, but because I am here, in my life.

I have realized that I am the love of my life. The biggest love story that can exist is the one you build with yourself. Love is magnetic; once you love yourself and surrender to it, it is impossible not to attract more love into your life.

The Dream

I have always been a big daydreamer. Daydreaming is my sanctuary for emotional exploration. It's a space where I relive cherished memories, reimagine past events, or envision scenarios that haven't come to fruition. Just as daydreaming does during waking hours, nighttime dreaming also creates a safe space for my mind to explore. One of my favorite dreams often takes me back to Rythmia.

During my first week at Rythmia, a beautiful wedding celebration took place one morning. It was a ceremony of two hearts. A declaration of their love and commitment to one another after a week of healing together.

That morning, I sat on my mattress and watched the ceremony in awe. It was so beautiful, simple, and genuine. I said to myself, "One day, I will walk that aisle."

My dream is so vivid that it feels like it has already happened. I am back at Rythmia. It's Friday morning. We have just finished the last all-night treatment of the week.

I am standing outside next to the fire, where I felt energy travel through my body for the first time. I am wearing one of Zeena's incredible designs. It is a beautiful white dress, spiritual and sexy, all at the same time.

I am holding sunflowers. They might be from new seeds, or perhaps they sprouted from those tiny seeds I planted in my head in Tulum, the ones that I wrapped in a wet paper towel just in case. The ones that told me that magic would happen if I opened my heart.

I am barefoot. I can see some of the people I love standing inside. They are smiling. As I start to walk, I feel tears rolling down my cheeks. They are happy tears, joyful tears. Tears of acknowledgment for the fact that life has gone in a full circle. I am standing in the place where my life once ended. This time, a new chapter is about to begin.

At that moment, I thank God for giving me a second chance at life in more ways than one and for guiding me to board the train of true love.

I hear my favorite musicians playing the songs I know by heart. The same melodies that carried me through my darkest hours. They are even more beautiful now.

I step in, and I see a man. He is waiting for me at the end of the aisle. I don't see his face yet; I always wake up when he is about to turn around.

CHAPTER 44
The Final Lessons

"When the student is ready the teacher will appear. When the student is truly ready... The teacher will disappear."

– Tao Te Ching

An image often crosses my mind: I'm five years old, twirling innocently and carelessly under the shade of my backyard's mandarin tree. My golden curls glistening in the sun, the wind caressing my skin. I'm laughing freely and joyfully.

A part of me wishes that I could tell her, "Everything will be alright; it will all work out. Be strong."

The other part of me feels like I have already told her this. Perhaps my future-self crossed the space and time barrier, and on that day, as I twirled, my heart got the message.

New Hiking Partners

I didn't deserve the childhood I got. However, I wouldn't change a thing if I was given the opportunity to be born again. It has been a strenuous yet magnificent hike. It has been my hike.

I'm still hiking through my Appalachian trail, and now that I can appreciate all its beauty, I hope to be far from Mount Katahdin, Maine, where the trail ends.

I am no longer hiking alone. I have my incredible family and my tribe walking alongside me. I am wearing better hiking shoes made out of joy and trust. My hiking sticks help to share the load of my weight more evenly. I call them love and compassion.

I allow the map of my past experiences to guide me, and I pay attention to the signposts and synchronicities along the way. When I reach each summit, I pause, breathe, smile, and take it all in for as long as possible.

There will always be some clouds on the horizon. Now I know that gratitude is the best protection against the storms.

Reclaiming Life

Over the last two years, I have learned how to feel. To feel like the child I once was, full of innocence, excitement, and hope. But with the experience and tools of an adult to process and forgive.

It is a gift to be able to feel and process all the human emotions we are here to feel. Emotions I had to tuck away so deep when I was a little girl, I didn't even know they were missing. All the love, the joy, the desire, the happiness, the heartbreak, and the fear.

Life was black and white until I dared to go to the darkest places of my mind with the help of the great mystery, God, the universe.

Each plant medicine and psychedelic treatment was crucial in bringing beautiful shades of colors into my life and in illuminating my path. They were the keys that helped me unlock the doors to my mind and heart.

Forgiveness

Some people say that the first step to healing is forgiveness. I disagree. That statement can push you to forgive too early. Forgiving too quickly can be an escapism tool, a way to invalidate and bypass the processing of your hurt.

Your patience and courage when processing all the emotions associated with traumatic experiences nudge you slowly towards forgiveness. The journey alone will bring tremendous emotional healing. Additional growth can come from forgiving as a last step.

It took me a year and a half to finally forgive my father. He betrayed me and broke my spirit, yet I forgave him. Not because he deserved it but because I have earned a life free of anger, resentment, and bitterness.

My forgiveness doesn't excuse his behavior. In stories, villains and heroes often have painful backgrounds. Both have experienced loss and heartache. They often grow up in dysfunctional families. But their paths diverge in how they respond to that pain and loss.

Hurt by the world, the villain seeks revenge. The hero, on the other hand, emerges with a heart to protect others from suffering. That choice defines their journey and shapes who they become. They have the power to shape their pain into a force for good or evil. They write the chapters of their own destinies and weave the tale of their souls.

I have compassion for the little boy my dad once was. He must have suffered in unimaginable ways in order to perpetuate this cycle of abuse as an adult. Yet, my adult father had a choice and he didn't choose the hero's path.

Justice was served a long time ago. He paid for his wrongdoing before he died. He was deeply unhappy his entire life. His heart was broken long before the bullets went in.

My Father, the Teacher

My father was my life's biggest teacher. He taught me how not to love. How not to treat a child. How not to live a life. He taught me all that I should not be. He played his role so I could embody mine.

He attempted to break me; instead, from the shattered pieces of my soul, I was able to rise as a much more compassionate woman than I would have ever been had I not survived what I went through.

I was ready for my father to appear during that fateful night in Costa Rica. Recovering my hidden memories revealed the darkness of his teachings. Yet, my memories also unlocked the door to a life of profound meaning and purpose.

There is no pursuit more worthy than tending to our own hearts and souls and extending a helping hand to others on their healing path.

My father's secret life came out of the shadows, and his legacy of trauma finally vanished into the full moon.

Through that disappearing act, I remembered who I am. Who I was always meant to be.

The small flicker that once struggled for survival in the heart of the little girl I once was is now an intense fire that burns brightly in my soul.

The journey to freedom may be challenging,

but the destination is a sanctuary no one can trespass

CHAPTER 45
Imagine the Future

"You may say I'm a dreamer, but I'm not the only one. I hope one day you'll join us, and the world will be as one."

– John Lennon

Imagine a future where the focus shifts from merely managing your struggles to understanding the deep-rooted causes of your challenges. You embrace the notion that your experiences, no matter how painful, hold the potential for growth and transformation.

In this future, mental health is seen as an integral part of your overall well-being, and seeking help is not stigmatized but encouraged. There is a culture of compassion, empathy, and understanding where you feel safe to share your story and find support in your healing process.

Therapists, healthcare providers, and spiritual guides work hand in hand to offer you a holistic approach to healing. They integrate the wisdom of traditional healing practices, such as plant medicine and meditation, with cutting-edge research in psychology and neuroscience.

In this future, you recognize the interconnectedness of all living beings and the impact of your healing on society as a whole. You value emotional intelligence and self-awareness as essential skills for creating healthy relationships and fostering a harmonious community.

As you journey towards this future, you let go of the notion that healing is a destination but understand it as an ongoing process of growth and self-discovery. You appreciate the ups and downs, the joys and challenges, knowing that each step forward brings you closer to your authentic self.

It's a future where we celebrate the beauty of our imperfections and embrace the full spectrum of human emotions.

The Shift

The seeds of metamorphosis have always been sown through the collective vision of dreamers and visionaries. The possibility of the future described above lies not only in the power of imagination but also in the tangible shifts already underway in our world.

Societies are witnessing a growing awareness and acceptance of mental health as a crucial aspect of overall well-being. Seeking help is being de-stigmatized. Holistic approaches to healing are being embraced and research is supporting the integration of traditional practices, psychedelics, and modern knowledge.

Moreover, the interconnectedness of our world has never been more evident. As individuals recognize the impact of their healing journey on the broader social fabric, a ripple effect of compassion and empathy spreads.

The transformative potential of such a future lies not only in its practical implications for mental health care but also in its resonance with the deepest yearnings of the human soul.

It offers a vision where we are no longer confined by our past traumas but empowered by the wisdom they bestow upon us. This future taps into our innate resilience and unlocks the vast reservoirs of human potential, sparking a renaissance of creativity, empathy, and understanding.

As the wave of change continues to build momentum, driven by brave individuals and progressive institutions, you find yourself standing at the threshold of an extraordinary era of growth and self-discovery.

By co-creating this reality, you sow the seeds of hope, resilience, and compassion for generations to come, ushering in an era where the power of your heart and mind reverberates through every corner of your existence, illuminating the very essence of what it means to be human.

Epilogue

"A good life is one hero journey after another."

-Joseph Campbell

If there was a time, while reading this book, when you found yourself comparing your journey to mine, please remember that each person's journey is unique. I constantly remind myself that life is not a race. Instead life is a dance between intention and surrender.

Setting clear intentions and goals allows you to take steps toward your desires. However, it's equally important for you to surrender to the flow of life. This openness allows for serendipitous encounters and further personal growth.

I don't think we are ever fully ready for anything in life. How boring would that be? You strive to be ready; eventually, you feel ready for something, and then you just wait for it to arrive? Odds are you will grow impatient and become "unready" once more.

The best parts of life happen when you are not ready. The universe loves to surprise you, to leave you in awe. Its signs and synchronicities encourage you to take a leap of faith.

Remembering the Future

Throughout our lives, we get messages. Some people think the messages come from God or the universe, others believe they come from their higher self, and others think they are from their subconscious mind.

The truth is that it doesn't matter where the messages originate or who they are from. We all get them, some of us dismiss them as a hunch, or we call them intuition. I believe the messages come to remind us of our future. It's up to us to listen or not.

We all can find answers or guidance by looking inwards, and sometimes when we do, magic happens.

Shortly after writing this book, I lay in bed one night and looked inward for guidance. A new thought came into my mind. I asked the universe:

"Is it time for my next hero journey, the one with the king of my heart by my side?"

I heard a voice answer in my head, "Yes, it is."

"Good," I whispered as I fell asleep.

Look Inward

If you have my book in your hands, you and I are connected by an invisible thread of love and resilience. My wish is that if your inner fire has gone out, you regained hope through my story.

Whether you choose to explore the depths of your consciousness through the lens of psychedelics or embark on a different path of introspection, the essence lies in your willingness to venture into the uncharted territories of your own being. It's about embracing vulnerability and daring to question your behaviors and emotions.

Whatever route you take, remember that you hold the paint brush, and the masterpiece you create is a testament to your resilience, your growth, and your capacity to embrace the unknown.

Step forward with the courage to explore, to seek, and transform. The canvas of your existence is vast and it's waiting to be painted with every heartbeat, with every thought, and with every choice you make.

More Praise

"Melissa is the epitome of survival against all odds. She masterfully expresses her vulnerability in the most genuine way. Most notably, Melissa taps into the effectiveness of almost every trauma based resource available to the public. This is a great service to anyone that is seeking comfort in a shared story. There is a benefit found for every person that picks up this book.

– Cheri L. Sotelo, Licensed Psychotherapist, Certified Family & Complex Trauma Specialist

"We're all about being a living legend and few people exemplify this like Melissa."

– Gerald Rogers

"From the moment I learned Melissa's story, helping and encouraging her to get it published was one of my top priorities. It will help you and change you in all the right ways."

– Maya Rose

"Not only is this a very helpful book for people who are dealing with trauma, but it is also a very easy book to read. You'll feel all the feelings and it's the kind of story that gets turned into a film."

– Jessica Sheehan

393

Final Thanks

To you, the reader - Thank you for embarking on this journey with me and for exploring the stories and insights shared. May you find reflections within these pages that serve as mirrors, allowing you to see and embrace all the facets of your own life and experiences.

To the mentors, speakers, writers, and all those who inspire - Thank you for being a candle in a dark room. Thank you for shining brightly and sharing your knowledge, experiences, and insights. Your light gave me hope when I felt lost and courage when I faced challenges.

To my Editor - Your expertise and commitment have been invaluable. Thank you for your insightful feedback and thoughtful suggestions; they helped me dig deeper and refine my thoughts.

To my Publisher - Thank you for understanding the heart and soul of my writing and for ensuring that my voice remained authentic throughout the publishing process. You have been a guiding force, providing expert advice and a keen eye for detail.

Made in the USA
Las Vegas, NV
23 February 2024

86179671R00221